This publication provides a general overview of a particular standards-related topic. This publication does not alter or determine compliance responsibilities which are set forth in OSHA standards, and the *Occupational Safety and Health Act of 1970*. Moreover, because interpretations and enforcement policy may change over time, for additional guidance on OSHA compliance requirements, the reader should consult current administrative interpretations and decisions by the Occupational Safety and Health Review Commission and the courts.

This information will be made available to sensory-impaired individuals upon request. Voice phone: (202) 693-1999; teletypewriter (TTY) number: 1-877-889-5627.

Laboratory Safety Guidance

Occupational Safety and Health Administration
U.S. Department of Labor

OSHA 3404-11R
2011

U.S. Department of Labor
Hilda L. Solis, Secretary of Labor

This guidance document is not a standard or regulation, and it creates no new legal obligations. It contains recommendations as well as descriptions of mandatory safety and health standards. The recommendations are advisory in nature, informational in content, and are intended to assist employers in providing a safe and healthful workplace. The *Occupational Safety and Health Act* requires employers to comply with safety and health standards and regulations promulgated by OSHA or by a state with an OSHA-approved state plan. In addition, the Act's General Duty Clause, Section 5(a)(1), requires employers to provide their employees with a workplace free from recognized hazards likely to cause death or serious physical harm.

OSHA®
**Occupational Safety and
Health Administration**

Contents

Introduction

More than 500,000 workers are employed in laboratories in the U.S. The laboratory environment can be a hazardous place to work. Laboratory workers are exposed to numerous potential hazards including chemical, biological, physical and radioactive hazards, as well as musculoskeletal stresses. Laboratory safety is governed by numerous local, state and federal regulations. Over the years, OSHA has promulgated rules and published guidance to make laboratories increasingly safe for personnel. This document is intended for supervisors, principal investigators and managers who have the primary responsibility for maintaining laboratories under their supervision as safe, healthy places to work and for ensuring that applicable health, safety and environmental regulations are followed. Worker guidance in the form of Fact Sheets and QuickCards™ is also provided for certain hazards that may be encountered in laboratories. There are several primary OSHA standards that apply to laboratories and these are discussed below. There are also other OSHA standards that apply to various aspects of laboratory activities and these are referred to in this document.

The Occupational Exposure to Hazardous Chemicals in Laboratories standard (29 CFR 1910.1450) was created specifically for non-production laboratories. Additional OSHA standards provide rules that protect workers, including those that who in laboratories, from chemical hazards as well as biological, physical and safety hazards. For those hazards that are not covered by a specific OSHA standard, OSHA often provides guidance on protecting workers from these hazards. This document is designed to make employers aware of the OSHA standards as well as OSHA guidance that is available to protect workers from the diverse hazards encountered in laboratories. The extent of detail on specific hazards provided in this document is dependent on the nature of each hazard and its importance in a laboratory setting. In addition to information on OSHA standards and guidance that deal with laboratory hazards, appendices are provided with information on other governmental and non-governmental agencies that deal with various aspects of laboratory safety.

This Laboratory Safety Guidance booklet deals specifically with laboratories within the jurisdiction of Federal OSHA. There are twenty-five states and two U.S. Territories (Puerto Rico and the Virgin Islands) that have their own OSHA-approved occupational safety and health standards, which may be different from federal standards, but must be at least "as effective as" the federal standards. Contact your local or state OSHA office for further information. More information on OSHA-approved state plans is available at: www.osha.gov/dcsp/osp/index.html.

OSHA Standards

Section 5(a)(1) of the *Occupational Safety and Health Act of 1970* (OSH Act), the **General Duty Clause**, requires that employers "shall furnish to each of his employees employment and a place of employment which are free from recognized hazards that are causing or likely to cause death or serious physical harm to his employees." Therefore, even if an OSHA standard has not been promulgated that deals with a specific hazard or hazardous operation, protection of workers from all hazards or hazardous operations may be enforceable under section 5(a)(1) of the OSH Act. For example, best practices that are issued by non-regulatory organizations such as the National Institute for Occupational Safety and Health (NIOSH), the Centers for Disease Control and Prevention (CDC), the National Research Council (NRC), and the National Institutes of Health (NIH), can be enforceable under section 5(a)(1).

The principal OSHA standards that apply to all non-production laboratories are listed below. Although this is not a comprehensive list, it includes standards that cover the major hazards that workers are most likely to encounter in their daily tasks. Employers must be fully aware of these standards and must implement all aspects of the standards that apply to specific laboratory work conditions in their facilities.

The Occupational Exposure to Hazardous Chemicals in Laboratories standard (29 CFR 1910.1450), commonly referred to as the Laboratory standard, requires that the employer designate a Chemical Hygiene Officer and have a written Chemical Hygiene Plan (CHP), and actively verify that it remains effective. The CHP must include provisions for worker training, chemical exposure monitoring where appropriate, medical consultation when exposure occurs, criteria for the use of personal protective equipment (PPE) and engineering controls, special precautions for particularly hazardous substances, and a requirement for a Chemical Hygiene Officer responsible for implementation of the CHP. The CHP must be tailored to reflect the specific chemical hazards present in the laboratory where it is to be used. Laboratory personnel must receive training regarding the Laboratory standard, the CHP, and other laboratory safety practices, including exposure detection, physical and health hazards associated with chemicals, and protective measures.

The Hazard Communication standard (29 CFR 1910.1200), sometimes called the HazCom standard, is a set of requirements first issued in 1983 by OSHA. The standard requires evaluating the potential hazards of chemicals, and communicating information concerning those hazards and appropriate protective measures to employees. The standard includes provisions for: developing and maintaining a written hazard communication program for the workplace, including lists of hazardous chemicals present; labeling of containers of chemicals in the workplace, as well as of containers of chemicals being shipped to other workplaces; preparation and distribution of material safety data sheets (MSDSs) to workers and downstream employers; and development and implementation of worker training programs regarding hazards of chemicals and protective measures. This OSHA standard requires manufacturers and importers of hazardous chemicals to provide material safety data sheets to users of the chemicals describing potential hazards and other information. They must also attach hazard warning labels to containers of the chemicals. Employers must make MSDSs available to workers. They must also train their workers in the hazards caused by the chemicals workers are exposed to and the appropriate protective measures that must be used when handling the chemicals.

The Bloodborne Pathogens standard (29 CFR 1910.1030), including changes mandated by the *Needlestick Safety and Prevention Act of 2001*, requires employers to protect workers from infection with human bloodborne pathogens in the workplace. The standard covers all workers with "reasonably anticipated" exposure to blood or other potentially infectious materials (OPIM). It requires that information and training be provided before the worker begins work that may involve occupational exposure to bloodborne pathogens, annually thereafter, and before a worker is offered hepatitis B vaccination. The Bloodborne Pathogens standard also requires advance information and training for all workers in research laboratories who handle human immunodeficiency virus (HIV) or hepatitis B virus (HBV). The standard was issued as a performance standard, which means that the employer must develop a written exposure control plan (ECP) to provide a safe and healthy work environment, but is allowed some flexibility in accomplishing this goal. Among other things, the ECP requires employers to make an exposure determination, establish procedures for evaluating incidents, and determine a schedule for implementing the standard's requirements, including engineering and work practice controls. The standard also requires employers to provide and pay for appropriate PPE for workers with occupational exposures. Although this standard only applies to bloodborne pathogens, the protective measures in this standard (e.g., ECP, engineering and work practice controls, administrative controls, PPE, housekeeping, training, post-exposure medical follow-up) are the same measures for effectively controlling exposure to other biological agents.

The Personal Protective Equipment (PPE) standard (29 CFR 1910.132) requires that employers provide and pay for PPE and ensure that it is used wherever "hazards of processes or environment, chemical hazards, radiological hazards, or mechanical irritants are encountered in a manner capable of causing injury or impairment in the function of any part of the body through absorption, inhalation or physical contact." [29 CFR 1910.132(a) and 1910.132(h)]. In order to determine whether and what PPE is needed, the employer must "assess the workplace to determine if hazards are present, or are likely to be present, which necessitate the use of [PPE]," 29 CFR 1910.132(d)(1). Based on that assessment, the employer must select appropriate PPE (e.g., protection for eyes, face, head, extremities; protective clothing; respiratory protection; shields and barriers) that will protect the affected worker from the hazard, 29 CFR 1910.132 (d)(1)(i), communicate selection decisions to each affected worker, 29 CFR 1910.132 (d)(1)(ii), and select PPE that properly fits each affected employee, 29 CFR 1910.132(d)(1)(iii). Employers must provide training for workers who are required to use PPE that addresses when and what PPE is necessary, how to wear and care for PPE properly, and the limitations of PPE, 29 CFR 1910.132(f).

The Eye and Face Protection standard (29 CFR 1910.133) requires employers to ensure that each affected worker uses appropriate eye or face protection when exposed to eye or face hazards from flying particles, molten metal, liquid chemicals, acids or caustic liquids, chemical gases or vapors, or potentially injurious light radiation, 29 CFR 1910.133(a).

The Respiratory Protection standard (29 CFR 1910.134) requires that a respirator be provided to each worker when such equipment is necessary to protect the health of such individual. The employer must provide respirators that are appropriate and suitable for the purpose intended, as described in 29 CFR 1910.134(d)(1). The employer is responsible for establishing and maintaining a respiratory protection program, as required by 29 CFR 1910.134(c), that includes, but is not limited to, the following: selection of respirators for use in the workplace; medical evaluations of workers required to use respirators; fit testing for tight-fitting respirators; proper use of respirators during routine and emergency situations; procedures and schedules for cleaning, disinfecting, storing, inspecting, repairing and discarding of respirators; procedures to ensure adequate air quality, quantity, and flow of breathing air for atmosphere-supplying respirators; training of workers in respiratory hazards that they may be exposed to during routine and emergency situations; training of workers in the proper donning and doffing of respirators, and any limitations on their use and maintenance; and regular evaluation of the effectiveness of the program.

The Hand Protection standard (29 CFR 1910.138), requires employers to select and ensure that workers use appropriate hand protection when their hands are exposed to hazards such as those from skin absorption of harmful substances; severe cuts or lacerations; severe abrasions; punctures; chemical burns; thermal burns; and harmful temperature extremes, 29 CFR 1910.138(a). Further, employers must base the selection of the appropriate hand protection on an evaluation of the performance characteristics of the hand protection relative to the task(s) to be performed, conditions present, duration of use, and the hazards and potential hazards identified, 29 CFR 1910.138(b).

The Control of Hazardous Energy standard (29 CFR 1910.147), often called the "Lockout/Tagout" standard, establishes basic requirements for locking and/or tagging out equipment while installation, maintenance, testing, repair, or construction operations are in progress. The primary purpose of the standard is to protect workers from the unexpected energization or startup of machines or equipment, or release of stored energy. The procedures apply to the shutdown of all potential energy sources associated with machines or equipment, including pressures, flows of fluids and gases, electrical power, and radiation.

In addition to the standards listed above, other OSHA standards that pertain to electrical safety

(29 CFR 1910 Subpart S-Electrical); fire safety (Portable Fire Extinguishers standard, 29 CFR 1910.157); and slips, trips and falls (29 CFR 1910 Subpart D – Walking-Working Surfaces, Subpart E - Means of Egress, and Subpart J - General Environmental Controls) are discussed at pages 25-28. These standards pertain to general industry, as well as laboratories. When laboratory workers are using large analyzers and other equipment, their potential exposure to electrical hazards associated with this equipment must be assessed by employers and appropriate precautions taken. Similarly, worker exposure to wet floors or spills and clutter can lead to slips/trips/falls and other possible injuries and employers must assure that these hazards are minimized. While large laboratory fires are rare, there is the potential for small bench-top fires, especially in laboratories using flammable solvents. It is the responsibility of employers to implement appropriate protective measures to assure the safety of workers.

Hierarchy of Controls

Occupational safety and health professionals use a framework called the "hierarchy of controls" to select ways of dealing with workplace hazards. The hierarchy of controls prioritizes intervention strategies based on the premise that the best way to control a hazard is to systematically remove it from the workplace, rather than relying on workers to reduce their exposure. The types of measures that may be used to protect laboratory workers, prioritized from the most effective to least effective, are:

- engineering controls;
- administrative controls;
- work practices; and
- personal protective equipment (PPE).

Most employers use a combination of control methods. Employers must evaluate their particular workplace to develop a plan for protecting their workers that may combine both immediate actions as well as longer term solutions. A description of each type of control for non-production laboratories follows.

Engineering controls are those that involve making changes to the work environment to reduce work-related hazards. These types of controls are preferred over all others because they make permanent changes that reduce exposure to hazards and do not rely on worker behavior. By reducing a hazard in the workplace, engineering controls can be the most cost-effective solutions for employers to implement.

Examples include:
- Chemical Fume Hoods; and
- Biological Safety Cabinets (BSCs).

Administrative controls are those that modify workers' work schedules and tasks in ways that minimize their exposure to workplace hazards.

Examples include:
- Developing a Chemical Hygiene Plan; and
- Developing Standard Operating Procedures for chemical handling.

Work practices are procedures for safe and proper work that are used to reduce the duration, frequency or intensity of exposure to a hazard. When defining safe work practice controls, it is a good idea for the employer to ask workers for their sug-

gestions, since they have firsthand experience with the tasks as actually performed. These controls need to be understood and followed by managers, supervisors and workers.

Examples include:
- No mouth pipetting; and
- Chemical substitution where feasible (e.g., selecting a less hazardous chemical for a specific procedure).

Personal Protective Equipment (PPE) is protective gear needed to keep workers safe while performing their jobs. Examples of PPE include respirators (for example, N95), face shields, goggles and disposable gloves. While engineering and administrative controls and proper work practices are considered to be more effective in minimizing exposure to many workplace hazards, the use of PPE is also very important in laboratory settings.

It is important that PPE be:
- Selected based upon the hazard to the worker;
- Properly fitted and in some cases periodically refitted (e.g., respirators);
- Conscientiously and properly worn;
- Regularly maintained and replaced in accord with the manufacturer's specifications;
- Properly removed and disposed of to avoid contamination of self, others or the environment; and
- If reusable, properly removed, cleaned, disinfected and stored.

> The following sections of this document are organized based upon classes of hazards, i.e., chemical, biological, physical, safety and other hazards. The organization of these sections and/or subsections may differ somewhat. For instance, OSHA's Laboratory standard is described in greater detail than any other standard in this document. This is because this is the only standard that is specific to laboratories (i.e., non-production laboratories). In all other sections, only those specific aspects of various standards that are considered most relevant to non-production laboratories are discussed. In sections of this document where there are no specific OSHA standards that apply, guidance in the form of Fact Sheets or QuickCards™ may be provided.

Chemical Hazards

Hazardous chemicals present physical and/or health threats to workers in clinical, industrial, and academic laboratories. Laboratory chemicals include cancer-causing agents (carcinogens), toxins (e.g., those affecting the liver, kidney, and nervous system), irritants, corrosives, sensitizers, as well as agents that act on the blood system or damage the lungs, skin, eyes, or mucous membranes. OSHA rules regulate exposures to approximately 400 substances.

Laboratory Standard (29 CFR 1910.1450)

In 1990, OSHA issued the Occupational Exposure to Hazardous Chemicals in Laboratories standard (29 CFR 1910.1450). Commonly known as the Laboratory standard, it was developed to address workplaces where relatively small quantities of hazardous chemicals are used on a non-production basis. However, not all laboratories are covered by the Laboratory standard. For example, most quality control laboratories are not covered under the standard. These laboratories are usually adjuncts of production operations which typically perform repetitive procedures for the purpose of assuring reliability of a product or a process. On the other hand, laboratories that conduct research and development and related analytical work are subject to the requirements of the Laboratory standard, regardless of whether or not they are used only to support manufacturing.

The purpose of the Laboratory standard is to ensure that workers in non-production laboratories are informed about the hazards of chemicals in their workplace and are protected from chemical exposures exceeding allowable levels [i.e., OSHA permissible exposure limits (PELs)] as specified in Table Z of the Air Contaminants standard (29 CFR 1910.1000) and as specified in other substance-specific health standards. The Laboratory standard achieves this protection by establishing safe work practices in laboratories to implement a Chemical Hygiene Plan (CHP).

Scope and Application

The Laboratory standard applies to all individuals engaged in laboratory use of hazardous chemicals. Work with hazardous chemicals outside of laboratories is covered by the Hazard Communication standard (29 CFR 1910.1200). Laboratory uses of chemicals which provide no potential for exposure (e.g., chemically impregnated test media or prepared kits for pregnancy testing) are not covered by the Laboratory standard.

Formaldehyde is one of the most commonly used hazardous chemicals in laboratories. The OSHA Formaldehyde standard (29 CFR 1910.1048) specifically deals with protecting workers from the hazards associated with exposure to this chemical. It should be noted that the scope of the Formaldehyde standard is not affected in most cases by the Laboratory standard. The Laboratory standard specifically does not apply to formaldehyde use in histology, pathology and human or animal anatomy laboratories; however, if formaldehyde is used in other types of laboratories which are covered by the Laboratory standard, the employer must comply with 29 CFR 1910.1450.

Program Description

The Laboratory standard consists of five major elements:
- Hazard identification;
- Chemical Hygiene Plan;
- Information and training;
- Exposure monitoring; and
- Medical consultation and examinations.

Each laboratory covered by the Laboratory standard must appoint a Chemical Hygiene Officer (CHO) to develop and implement a Chemical Hygiene Plan. The CHO is responsible for duties such as monitoring processes, procuring chemicals, helping project directors upgrade facilities, and advising administrators on improved chemical hygiene policies and practices. A worker designated as the CHO must be qualified, by training or experience, to provide technical guidance in developing and implementing the provisions of the CHP.

Hazard Identification

Each laboratory must identify which hazardous chemicals will be encountered by its workers. All containers for chemicals must be clearly labeled. An employer must ensure that workers do not use, store, or allow any other person to use or store, any hazardous substance in his or her laboratory if the container does not meet the labeling requirements outlined in the Hazard Communication standard,

29 CFR 1910.1200(f)(4). Labels on chemical containers must not be removed or defaced.

Material Safety Data Sheets (MSDSs) for chemicals received by the laboratory must be supplied by the manufacturer, distributor, or importer and must be maintained and readily accessible to laboratory workers. MSDSs are written or printed materials concerning a hazardous chemical. Employers must have an MSDS in the workplace for each hazardous chemical in use.

MSDS sheets must contain:
1. Name of the chemical;
2. Manufacturer's information;
3. Hazardous ingredients/identity information;
4. Physical/chemical characteristics;
5. Fire and explosion hazard data;
6. Reactivity data;
7. Health hazard data;
8. Precautions for safe handling and use; and
9. Control measures.

The United States is participating in the Global Harmonization System of Classifying and Labeling Chemicals (GHS) process and is planning to adopt the GHS in its Hazard Communication standard. The GHS process is designed to improve comprehensibility, and thus the effectiveness of the Hazard Communication standard (HCS), and help to further reduce illnesses and injuries. GHS is a system that defines and classifies the hazards of chemical products, and communicates health and safety information on labels and material safety data sheets (called Safety Data Sheets, or SDSs, in the GHS). The most significant changes to the Hazard Communication standard will include changing terminology: "hazard determination" to "hazard classification" (along with related terms) and "material safety data sheet" to "safety data sheet." The goal is that the same set of rules for classifying hazards, and the same format and content for labels and safety data sheets (SDS) will be adopted and used around the world. An international team of hazard communication experts developed GHS.

The biggest visible impact of the GHS is the appearance of and information required for labels and SDSs. Labels will require signal words, pictograms, precautionary statements and appropriate hazard statements. The GHS system covers all hazardous chemicals and may be adopted to cover chemicals in the workplace, transport, consumer products, and pesticides. SDSs will follow a new 16-section format, containing requirements similar to those identified in the American National Standards Institute (ANSI) Z400 and International Organization for Standardization (ISO) 11014 standards. Information on GHS classification, labels and SDSs is available at: http://www.unece.org/trans/danger/publi/ghs/ghs_welcome_e.html.

Chemical Hygiene Plan (CHP)

The purpose of the CHP is to provide guidelines for prudent practices and procedures for the use of chemicals in the laboratory. The Laboratory standard requires that the CHP set forth procedures, equipment, PPE and work practices capable of protecting workers from the health hazards presented by chemicals used in the laboratory.

The following information must be included in each CHP:

Standard Operating Procedures (SOPs): Prudent laboratory practices which must be followed when working with chemicals in a laboratory. These include general and laboratory-specific procedures for work with hazardous chemicals.

Criteria for Exposure Control Measures: Criteria used by the employer to determine and implement control measures to reduce worker exposure to hazardous chemicals including engineering controls, the use of PPE and hygiene practices.

Adequacy and Proper Functioning of Fume Hoods and other Protective Equipment: Specific measures that must be taken to ensure proper and adequate performance of protective equipment, such as fume hoods.

Information and Training: The employer must provide information and training required to ensure that workers are apprised of the hazards of chemicals in their work areas and related information.

Requirement of Prior Approval of Laboratory Procedures: The circumstances under which certain laboratory procedures or activities require approval from the employer or employer's designee before work is initiated.

Medical Consultations and Examinations: Provisions for medical consultation and examination when exposure to a hazardous chemical has or may have taken place.

Occupational Safety and Health Administration

Chemical Hygiene Officer Designation: Identification of the laboratory CHO and outline of his or her role and responsibilities; and, where appropriate, establishment of a Chemical Hygiene Committee.

Particularly Hazardous Substances: Outlines additional worker protections for work with particularly hazardous substances. These include select carcinogens, reproductive toxins, and substances which have a high degree of acute toxicity.

Information and Training

Laboratory workers must be provided with information and training relevant to the hazards of the chemicals present in their laboratory. The training must be provided at the time of initial assignment to a laboratory and prior to assignments involving new exposure situations.

The employer must inform workers about the following:

- The content of the OSHA Laboratory standard and its appendices (the full text must be made available);
- The location and availability of the Chemical Hygiene Plan;
- Permissible exposure limits (PELs) for OSHA-regulated substances, or recommended exposure levels for other hazardous chemicals where there is no applicable standard;
- Signs and symptoms associated with exposure to hazardous chemicals in the laboratory; and
- The location and availability of reference materials on the hazards, safe handling, storage and disposal of hazardous chemicals in the laboratory, including, but not limited to, MSDSs.

Training must include the following:

- Methods and observations used to detect the presence or release of a hazardous chemical. These may include employer monitoring, continuous monitoring devices, and familiarity with the appearance and odor of the chemicals;
- The physical and health hazards of chemicals in the laboratory work area;
- The measures that workers can take to protect themselves from these hazards, including protective equipment, appropriate work practices, and emergency procedures;
- Applicable details of the employer's written Chemical Hygiene Plan;
- Retraining, if necessary.

Exposure Determination

OSHA has established permissible exposure limits (PELs), as specified in 29 CFR 1910, subpart Z, for hundreds of chemical substances. A PEL is the chemical-specific concentration in inhaled air that is intended to represent what the average, healthy worker may be exposed to daily for a lifetime of work without significant adverse health effects. The employer must ensure that workers' exposures to OSHA-regulated substances do not exceed the PEL. However, most of the OSHA PELs were adopted soon after the Agency was first created in 1970 and were based upon scientific studies available at that time. Since science has continued to move forward, in some cases, there may be health data that suggests a hazard to workers below the levels permitted by the OSHA PELs. Other agencies and organizations have developed and updated recommended occupational exposure limits (OELs) for chemicals regulated by OSHA, as well as other chemicals not currently regulated by OSHA. Employers should consult other OELs, in addition to the OSHA PEL, to make a fully informed decision about the potential health risks to workers associated with chemical exposures. The American Conference of Governmental Industrial Hygienists (ACGIH), the American Industrial Hygiene Association (AIHA), the National Institute for Occupational Safety and Health (NIOSH), as well as some chemical manufacturers have established OELs to assess safe exposure limits for various chemicals.

Employers must conduct exposure monitoring, through air sampling, if there is reason to believe that workers may be exposed to chemicals above the action level or, in the absence of an action level, the PEL. Periodic exposure monitoring should be conducted in accord with the provisions of the relevant standard. The employer should notify workers of the results of any monitoring within 15 working days of receiving the results. Some OSHA chemical standards have specific provisions regarding exposure monitoring and worker notification. Employers should consult relevant standards to see if these provisions apply to their workplace.

Medical Consultations and Examinations

Employers must do the following:

- Provide all exposed workers with an opportunity to receive medical attention by a licensed physician, including any follow-up examinations which the examining physician determines to be necessary.

- Provide an opportunity for a medical consultation by a licensed physician whenever a spill, leak, explosion or other occurrence results in the likelihood that a laboratory worker experienced a hazardous exposure in order to determine whether a medical examination is needed.
- Provide an opportunity for a medical examination by a licensed physician whenever a worker develops signs or symptoms associated with a hazardous chemical to which he or she may have been exposed in the laboratory.
- Establish medical surveillance for a worker as required by the particular standard when exposure monitoring reveals exposure levels routinely exceeding the OSHA action level or, in the absence of an action level, the PEL for an OSHA regulated substance.
- Provide the examining physician with the identity of the hazardous chemical(s) to which the individual may have been exposed, and the conditions under which the exposure may have occurred, including quantitative data, where available, and a description of the signs and symptoms of exposure the worker may be experiencing.
- Provide all medical examinations and consultations without cost to the worker, without loss of pay, and at a reasonable time and place.

The examining physician must complete a written opinion that includes the following information:
- Recommendations for further medical follow-up.
- The results of the medical examination and any associated tests.
- Any medical condition revealed in the course of the examination that may place the individual at increased risk as a result of exposure to a hazardous chemical in the workplace.
- A statement that the worker has been informed of the results of the consultation or medical examination and any medical condition that may require further examination or treatment. However, the written opinion must not reveal specific findings of diagnoses unrelated to occupational exposure.

A copy of the examining physician's written opinion must be provided to the exposed worker.

Recordkeeping
Employers must also maintain an accurate record of exposure monitoring activities and exposure measurements as well as medical consultations and examinations, including medical tests and written opinions. Employers generally must maintain worker exposure records for 30 years and medical records for the duration of the worker's employment plus 30 years, unless one of the exemptions listed in 29 CFR 1910.1020(d)(1)(i)(A)-(C) applies. Such records must be maintained, transferred, and made available, in accord with 29 CFR 1910.1020, to an individual's physician or made available to the worker or his/her designated representative upon request.

Roles and Responsibilities in Implementing the Laboratory Standard
The following are the National Research Council's recommendations concerning the responsibilities of various individuals for chemical hygiene in laboratories.

Chief Executive Officer
- Bears ultimate responsibility for chemical hygiene within the facility.
- Provides continuing support for institutional chemical hygiene.

Chemical Hygiene Officer
- Develops and implements appropriate chemical hygiene policies and practices.
- Monitors procurement, use, and disposal of chemicals used in the lab.
- Ensures that appropriate audits are maintained.
- Helps project directors develop precautions and adequate facilities.
- Knows the current legal requirements concerning regulated substances.
- Seeks ways to improve the chemical hygiene program.

Laboratory Supervisors
- Have overall responsibility for chemical hygiene in the laboratory.
- Ensure that laboratory workers know and follow the chemical hygiene rules.
- Ensure that protective equipment is available and in working order.
- Ensure that appropriate training has been provided.
- Provide regular, formal chemical hygiene and housekeeping inspections, including routine inspections of emergency equipment.
- Know the current legal requirements concerning regulated substances.
- Determine the required levels of PPE and equipment.

- Ensure that facilities and training for use of any material being ordered are adequate.

Laboratory Workers
- Plan and conduct each operation in accord with the facility's chemical hygiene procedures, including use of PPE and engineering controls, as appropriate.
- Develop good personal chemical hygiene habits.
- Report all accidents and potential chemical exposures immediately.

For more detailed information, OSHA has developed a Safety and Health Topics Page on Laboratories available at: www.osha.gov/SLTC/laboratories/index.html. See the Appendix for other OSHA documents relevant to this topic.

Two OSHA Fact Sheets have been developed to supplement this section. One is entitled **Laboratory Safety – OSHA Laboratory Standard**, and the other is entitled **Laboratory Safety – Chemical Hygiene Plan**; both are available online at www.osha.gov.

Hazard Communication Standard (29 CFR 1910.1200)

This standard is designed to protect against chemical source illnesses and injuries by ensuring that employers and workers are provided with sufficient information to recognize, evaluate and control chemical hazards and take appropriate protective measures.

The steps that employers must take to comply with the requirements of this standard must include, but are not limited to:
- Development and maintenance of a written hazard communication program for the workplace, including lists of hazardous chemicals present;
- Ensuring that containers of chemicals in the workplace, as well as containers of chemicals being shipped to other workplaces, are properly labeled;
- Ensuring that material safety data sheets (MSDSs) for chemicals that workers may be exposed to are made available to workers; and
- Development and implementation of worker training programs regarding hazards of chemicals they may be exposed to and the appropriate protective measures that must be used when handling these chemicals.

This OSHA standard also requires manufacturers and importers of hazardous chemicals to provide MSDSs to users of the chemicals describing potential hazards and other information. They must also attach hazard warning labels to containers of the chemicals. Distributors of hazardous chemicals must also provide MSDSs to employers and other distributors.

An OSHA QuickFacts entitled **Laboratory Safety – Labeling and Transfer of Chemicals** has been developed to supplement this section and is available online at www.osha.gov.

Specific Chemical Hazards
Air Contaminants standard (29 CFR 1910.1000)

The Air Contaminants standard provides rules for protecting workers from airborne exposure to over 400 chemicals. Several of these chemicals are commonly used in laboratories and include: toluene, xylene, and acrylamide. Toluene and xylene are solvents used to fix tissue specimens and rinse stains. They are primarily found in histology, hematology, microbiology and cytology laboratories.

Toluene		
Exposure routes	**Symptoms**	**Target Organs**
Inhalation; Ingestion; Skin and/or eye contact; Skin absorption.	Irritation of eyes, nose; Weakness, exhaustion, confusion, euphoria, headache; Dilated pupils, tearing; Anxiety; Muscle fatigue; Insomnia; Tingling, pricking, or numbness of skin; Dermatitis; Liver, kidney damage.	Eyes; Skin; Respiratory system; Central nervous system; Liver; Kidneys.

Xylene		
Exposure routes	**Symptoms**	**Target Organs**
Inhalation; Ingestion; Skin and/or eye contact; Skin absorption.	Irritation of eyes, skin, nose, throat; Dizziness, excitement, drowsiness, incoherence, staggering gait; Corneal vacuolization (cell debris); Anorexia, nausea, vomiting, abdominal pain; Dermatitis.	Eyes; Skin; Respiratory system; Central nervous system; GI tract; Blood; Liver; Kidneys.

Acrylamide is usually found in research laboratories and is used to make polyacrylamide gels for separations of macromolecules (e.g., DNA, proteins).

Acrylamide		
Exposure routes	**Symptoms**	**Target Organs**
Inhalation; Ingestion; Skin and/or eye contact; Skin absorption.	Irritation of eyes, skin; Ataxia (staggering gait), numb limbs, tingling, pricking, or numbness of skin; Muscle weakness; Absence of deep tendon reflex; Hand sweating; Tearing, Drowsiness; Reproductive effects; Potential occupational carcinogen.	Eyes; Skin; Central nervous system; Peripheral nervous system; Reproductive system (in animals: tumors of the lungs, testes, thyroid and adrenal glands).

Employers must do the following to prevent worker exposure:

Implement a written program for chemicals that workers are exposed to and that meet the requirements of the Hazard Communication standard. This program must contain provisions for worker training, warning labels and access to Material Safety Data Sheets (MSDSs).

Formaldehyde standard (29 CFR 1910.1048)

Formaldehyde is used as a fixative and is commonly found in most laboratories. The employer must ensure that no worker is exposed to an airborne concentration of formaldehyde which exceeds 0.75 parts formaldehyde per million parts of air (0.75 ppm) as an 8-hour time weighted average (TWA), 29 CFR 1910.1048(c)(1).

The Hazard Communication standard requires employers to maintain an MSDS, which manufacturers or distributors of formaldehyde are required to provide. The MSDS must be kept in an area that is accessible to workers that may be exposed to formaldehyde.

Formaldehyde		
Exposure routes	**Symptoms**	**Target Organs**
Inhalation; Ingestion; Skin and/or eye contact.	Irritation of eyes, skin, nose, throat, respiratory system; Tearing; Coughing; Wheezing; Dermatitis; Potential occupational nasal carcinogen.	Eyes; Skin; Respiratory system.

Employers must provide the following to workers to prevent exposure:

- Appropriate PPE, 29 CFR 1910.132, 29 CFR 1910.133, and 29 CFR 1910.1048(h).
- Acceptable eyewash facilities within the immediate work area for emergency use, if there is any possibility that a worker's eyes may be splashed with solutions containing 0.1 percent or greater formaldehyde, 29 CFR 1910.1048(i)(3).

Latex

One of the most common chemicals that laboratory workers are exposed to is latex, a plant protein. The most common cause of latex allergy is direct contact with latex, a natural plant derivative used in making certain disposable gloves and other products. Some healthcare workers have been determined to be latex sensitive, with reactions ranging from localized dermatitis (skin irritation) to immediate, possibly life-threatening reactions. Under OSHA's Personal Protective Equipment standard, 29 CFR 1910.132, the employer must ensure that appropriate personal protective equipment (PPE) is accessible at the worksite or issued to workers. Latex-free gloves, glove liners, powder-free gloves, or other similar alternatives are obtainable and must be readily accessible to those workers who are allergic to latex gloves or other latex-containing PPE, 29 CFR 1910.1030(c)(3)(iii).

Latex allergy should be suspected in workers who develop certain symptoms after latex exposure, including:

- nasal, eye, or sinus irritation
- hives or rash
- difficulty breathing
- coughing
- wheezing
- nausea
- vomiting
- diarrhea

An exposed worker who exhibits these symptoms should be evaluated by a physician or other licensed healthcare professional because further exposure could cause a serious allergic reaction.

Once a worker becomes allergic to latex, special precautions are needed to prevent exposures. Certain medications may reduce the allergic symptoms, but complete latex avoidance is the most effective approach.

Appropriate work practices should be used to reduce the chance of reactions to latex. If a worker must wear latex gloves, oil-based hand creams or lotions (which can cause glove deterioration) should not be used unless they have been shown to reduce latex-related problems and maintain glove barrier protection. After removing latex gloves, workers should wash their hands with a mild soap and dry them thoroughly.

An OSHA QuickFacts entitled **Laboratory Safety – Latex Allergy** has been developed to supplement this section and is available online at www.osha.gov.

Specific Engineering Control - Chemical Fume Hoods

The fume hood is often the primary control device for protecting laboratory workers when working with flammable and/or toxic chemicals. OSHA's Occupational Exposure to Hazardous Chemicals in Laboratories standard, 29 CFR 1910.1450, requires that fume hoods be maintained and function properly when used, 29 CFR 1910.1450(e)(3)(iii).

An OSHA QuickFacts entitled **Laboratory Safety – Chemical Fume Hoods** has been developed to supplement this section and is available online at www.osha.gov.

Biological Hazards

Biological Agents (other than Bloodborne Pathogens) and Biological Toxins

Many laboratory workers encounter daily exposure to biological hazards. These hazards are present in various sources throughout the laboratory such as blood and body fluids, culture specimens, body tissue and cadavers, and laboratory animals, as well as other workers.

A number of OSHA's Safety and Health Topics Pages mentioned below have information on select agents and toxins. These are federally regulated biological agents (e.g., viruses, bacteria, fungi, and prions) and toxins that have the potential to pose a severe threat to public health and safety, to animal or plant health, or to animal or plant products. The agents and toxins that affect animal and plant health are also referred to as high-consequence livestock pathogens and toxins, non-overlap agents and toxins, and listed plant pathogens. Select agents and toxins are defined by lists that appear in sections 73.3 of Title 42 of the Code of Federal Regulations (HHS/CDC *Select Agent Regulations*), sections 121.3 and 121.4 of Title 9 of the Code of Federal Regulations (USDA/APHIS/VS Select Agent Regulations), and section 331.3 of Title 7 of the Code of Federal Regulations (plants - USDA/APHIS/PPQ *Select Agent Regulations*) and Part 121, Title 9, Code of Federal Regulations (animals – USDA/APHIS). Select agents and toxins that are regulated by both HHS/CDC and USDA/APHIS are referred to as "overlap" select agents and toxins (see 42 CFR section 73.4 and 9 CFR 121.4).

Employers may use the list below as a starting point for technical and regulatory information about some of the most virulent and prevalent biological agents and toxins. The OSHA Safety and Health Topics Page entitled Biological Agents can be accessed at: www.osha.gov/SLTC/biologicalagents/index.html.

Anthrax. Anthrax is an acute infectious disease caused by a spore-forming bacterium called *Bacillus anthracis*. It is generally acquired following contact with anthrax-infected animals or anthrax-contaminated animal products. ***Bacillus anthracis* is an HHS and USDA select agent.**

Avian Flu. Avian influenza is caused by Influenza A viruses. These viruses normally reside in the intestinal tracts of water fowl and shore birds, where they cause little, if any, disease. However, when they are passed on to domestic birds, such as chickens, they can cause deadly contagious disease, highly pathogenic avian influenza (HPAI). **HPAI viruses are considered USDA/APHIS select agents.**

Botulism. Cases of botulism are usually associated with consumption of preserved foods. However, botulinum toxins are currently among the most common compounds explored by terrorists for use as biological weapons. **Botulinum neurotoxins, the causative agents of botulism, are HHS/CDC select agents.**

Foodborne Disease. Foodborne illnesses are caused by viruses, bacteria, parasites, toxins, metals, and prions (microscopic protein particles). Symptoms range from mild gastroenteritis to life-threatening neurologic, hepatic and renal syndromes.

Hantavirus. Hantaviruses are transmitted to humans from the dried droppings, urine, or saliva of mice and rats. Animal laboratory workers and persons working in infested buildings are at increased risk to this disease.

Legionnaires' Disease. Legionnaires' disease is a bacterial disease commonly associated with water-based aerosols. It is often the result of poorly maintained air conditioning cooling towers and potable water systems.

Molds and Fungi. Molds and fungi produce and release millions of spores small enough to be air-, water-, or insect-borne which may have negative effects on human health including, allergic reactions, asthma, and other respiratory problems.

Plague. The World Health Organization reports 1,000 to 3,000 cases of plague every year. A bioterrorist release of plague could result in a rapid spread of the pneumonic form of the disease, which could have devastating consequences. ***Yersinia pestis*, the causative agent of plague, is an HHS/CDC select agent.**

Ricin. Ricin is one of the most toxic and easily produced plant toxins. It has been used in the past as a bioterrorist weapon and remains a serious threat. **Ricin is an HHS/CDC select toxin.**

Severe Acute Respiratory Syndrome (SARS). SARS is an emerging, sometimes fatal, respiratory illness. According to the Centers for Disease Control and Prevention (CDC), the most recent human cases of SARS were reported in China in April 2004 and there is currently no known transmission anywhere in the world.

Smallpox. Smallpox is a highly contagious disease unique to humans. It is estimated that no more than 20 percent of the population has any immunity from previous vaccination. **Variola major virus, the causative agent for smallpox, is an HHS/CDC select agent.**

Tularemia. Tularemia is also known as "rabbit fever" or "deer fly fever" and is extremely infectious. Relatively few bacteria are required to cause the disease, which is why it is an attractive weapon for use in bioterrorism. ***Francisella tularensis*, the causative agent for tularemia, is an HHS/CDC select agent.**

Viral Hemorrhagic Fevers (VHFs). Hemorrhagic fever viruses are among the agents identified by the Centers for Disease Control and Prevention (CDC) as the most likely to be used as biological weapons. Many VHFs can cause severe, life-threatening disease with high fatality rates. **Many VHFs are HHS/CDC select agents; for example, Marburg virus, Ebola viruses, and the Crimean-Congo hemorrhagic fever virus.**

An additional OSHA Safety and Health Topics page on Pandemic Influenza has been added in response to the 2009 H1N1 influenza pandemic. It can be accessed at: www.osha.gov/dsg/topics/pandemicflu/index.html.

Pandemic Influenza. A pandemic is a global disease outbreak. An influenza pandemic occurs when a new influenza virus emerges for which there is little or no immunity in the human population; begins to cause serious illness; and then spreads easily person-to-person worldwide.

> The list above does not include all of the biological agents and toxins that may be hazardous to laboratory workers. New agents will be added over time. For agents that may pose a hazard to laboratory workers but are not listed above, consult the CDC web page at: www.cdc.gov. See Appendix for more information on BSL levels.

Material Safety Data Sheets (MSDSs) on Infectious Agents

Although MSDSs for chemical products have been available to workers for many years in the U.S. and other countries, Canada is the only country that has developed MSDSs for infectious agents. These MSDSs were produced by the Canadian Public Health Agency for personnel working in the life sciences as quick safety reference material relating to infectious microorganisms.

These MSDSs on Infectious Agents are organized to contain health hazard information such as infectious dose, viability (including decontamination), medical information, laboratory hazard, recommended precautions, handling information and spill procedures. These MSDSs are available at: www.phac-aspc.gc.ca/msds-ftss.

Bloodborne Pathogens

The OSHA Bloodborne Pathogens (BBP) standard (29 CFR 1910.1030) is designed to protect workers from the health hazards of exposure to bloodborne pathogens. Employers are subject to the BBP standard if they have workers whose jobs put them at reasonable risk of coming into contact with blood or other potentially infectious materials (OPIM). Employers subject to this standard must develop a written Exposure Control Plan, provide training to exposed workers, and comply with other requirements of the standard, including use of Standard Precautions when dealing with blood and OPIM. In 2001, in response to the *Needlestick Safety and Prevention Act*, OSHA revised the Bloodborne Pathogens standard. The revised standard clarifies the need for employers to select safer needle devices and to involve workers in identifying and choosing these devices. The updated standard also requires employers to maintain a log of injuries from contaminated sharps.

OSHA estimates that 5.6 million workers in the healthcare industry and related occupations are at risk of occupational exposure to bloodborne pathogens, including HIV, HBV, HCV, and others. All occupational exposure to blood or OPIM places workers at risk for infection with bloodborne pathogens. OSHA defines blood to mean human blood, human blood components, and products made from human blood. OPIM means: (1) The following human body fluids: semen, vaginal secretions, cerebrospinal fluid, synovial fluid, pleural fluid, pericardial fluid, peritoneal fluid, amniotic fluid, saliva in dental procedures, any body fluid that is visibly contaminated with blood, and all body fluids in situations where it is difficult or impossible to differentiate between body fluids; (2) Any unfixed tissue or organ (other than intact skin) from a human (living or dead); and (3) HIV- or HBV-containing cell or tissue cultures, organ cultures, and HIV- or HBV-containing culture medium or other solutions; and blood, organs, or other tissues from experimental animals infected with HIV or HBV.

The Centers for Disease Control and Prevention (CDC) notes that although more than 200 different diseases can be transmitted from exposure to blood, the most serious infections are hepatitis B virus (HBV), hepatitis C virus (HCV), and human immunodeficiency virus (HIV). Fortunately, the risk of acquiring any of these infections is low. HBV is the most infectious virus of the three viruses listed above. For an unvaccinated healthcare worker, the risk of developing an infection from a single needlestick or a cut exposed to HBV-infected blood ranges from 6-30%. The risk for infection from HCV- and HIV-infected blood under the same circumstances is 1.8 and 0.3 percent, respectively. This means that after a needlestick/cut exposure to HCV-contaminated blood, 98.2% of individuals do not become infected, while after a similar exposure to HIV-contaminated blood, 99.7% of individuals do not become infected. (http://www.cdc.gov/OralHealth/infectioncontrol/faq/bloodborne_exposures.htm).

Many factors influence the risk of becoming infected after a needlestick or cut exposure to HBV-, HCV- or HIV-contaminated blood. These factors include the health status of the individual, the volume of the blood exchanged, the concentration of the virus in the blood, the extent of the cut or the depth of penetration of the needlestick, etc.

Employers must ensure that workers are trained and prohibited from engaging in the following activities:

- Mouth pipetting/suctioning of blood or OPIM, 29 CFR 1910.1030(d)(2)(xii);
- Eating, drinking, smoking, applying cosmetics or lip balm, or handling contact lenses in work areas where there is a reasonable likelihood of occupational exposure to blood or OPIM, 29 CFR 1910.1030(d)(2)(ix); and
- Storage of food or drink in refrigerators, freezers, shelves, cabinets or on countertops or benchtops where blood or OPIM are present, 29 CFR 1910.1030(d)(2)(x).

Employers must ensure that the following are provided:

- Appropriate PPE for workers if blood or OPIM exposure is anticipated, 29 CFR 1910.1030(d)(3);
  - The type and amount of PPE depends on the anticipated exposure.
    - Gloves must be worn when hand contact with blood, mucous membranes, OPIM, or non-intact skin is anticipated, or when handling contaminated items or surfaces, 29 CFR 1910.1030(d)(3)(ix).
    - Surgical caps or hoods and/or shoe covers or boots must be worn in instances when gross contamination can reasonably be anticipated such as during autopsies or orthopedic surgery, 29 CFR 1910.1030(d)(3)(xii).
- Effective engineering and work practice controls to help remove or isolate exposures to blood and bloodborne pathogens, 29 CFR 1910.1030(d)(2)(i), CPL 02-02-069 (CPL 2-2.69); and
- Hepatitis B vaccination (if not declined by a worker) under the supervision of a physician or other licensed healthcare professional to all workers who have occupational exposure to blood or OPIM, 29 CFR 1910.1030(f)(1)(ii)(A)-(C).

Labels

When any blood, OPIM or infected animals are present in the work area, a hazard warning sign (see graphic) incorporating the universal biohazard symbol, 29 CFR 1910.1030(g)(1)(ii)(A), must be posted on all access doors, 29 CFR 1910.1030(e)(2)(ii)(D).

Engineering Controls and Work Practices for All HIV/HBV Laboratories

BIOHAZARD

Employers must ensure that:

- All activities involving OPIM are conducted in Biological Safety Cabinets (BSCs) or other physical-containment devices; work with OPIM must not be conducted on the open bench, 29 CFR 1910.1030(e)(2)(ii)(E);
- Certified BSCs or other appropriate combinations of personal protection or physical containment devices, such as special protective clothing, respirators, centrifuge safety cups, sealed centrifuge rotors, and containment caging for animals, be used for all activities with OPIM that pose a threat of exposure to droplets, splashes, spills, or aerosols, 29 CFR 1910.1030(e)(2)(iii)(A);
- Each laboratory contains a facility for hand washing and an eyewash facility which is readily available within the work area, 29 CFR 1910.1030(e)(3)(i); and
- Each work area contains a sink for washing hands and a readily available eyewash facility. The sink must be foot, elbow, or automatically operated and must be located near the exit door of the work area, 29 CFR 1910.1030(e)(4)(iii).

Additional BBP Standard Requirements Apply to HIV and HBV Research Laboratories

Requirements include:
- Waste materials:
  - All regulated waste must either be incinerated or decontaminated by a method such as autoclaving known to effectively destroy bloodborne pathogens, 29 CFR 1910.1030(e)(2)(i); and
  - Contaminated materials that are to be decontaminated at a site away from the work area must be placed in a durable, leakproof, labeled or color-coded container that is closed before being removed from the work area, 29 CFR 1910.1030(e)(2)(ii)(B).
- Access:
  - Laboratory doors must be kept closed when work involving HIV or HBV is in progress, 29 CFR 1910.1030(e)(2)(ii)(A);
  - Access to the production facilities' work area must be limited to authorized persons. Written policies and procedures must be established whereby only persons who have been advised of the potential biohazard, who

OSHA
Occupational Safety and
Health Administration

meet any specific entry requirements, and who comply with all entry and exit procedures must be allowed to enter the work areas and animal rooms, 29 CFR 1910.1030(e)(2)(ii)(C);

- Access doors to the production facilities' work area or containment module must be self-closing, 29 CFR 1910.1030(e)(4)(iv);

- Work areas must be separated from areas that are open to unrestricted traffic flow within the building. Passage through two sets of doors must be the basic requirement for entry into the work area from access corridors or other contiguous areas. Physical separation of the high-containment work area from access corridors or other areas or activities may also be provided by a double-doored clothes-change room (showers may be included), airlock, or other access facility that requires passing through two sets of doors before entering the work area, 29 CFR 1910.1030(e)(4)(i); and

- The surfaces of doors, walls, floors and ceilings in the work area must be water-resistant so that they can be easily cleaned. Penetrations in these surfaces must be sealed or capable of being sealed to facilitate decontamination, 29 CFR 1910.1030(e)(4)(ii).

(These requirements **do not apply** to clinical or diagnostic laboratories engaged solely in the analysis of blood, tissue, or organs, 29 CFR 1910.1030(e)(1).)

Research Animals

All procedures on animals should be performed by properly trained personnel. By using safe work practices and appropriate PPE, 29 CFR 1910.132(a), workers can minimize the likelihood that they will be bitten, scratched, and/or exposed to animal body fluids and tissues.

Possible Injuries/Illnesses

The most common work-related health complaints reported by individuals working with small animals are the following:
1. Sprains;
2. Strains;
3. Bites; and
4. Allergies.

Of these injuries, allergies (i.e., exaggerated reactions by the body's immune system) to proteins in small animals' urine, saliva, and dander are the greatest potential health risk. An allergic response may evolve into life-long asthma. Because mice and rats are the animals most frequently used in

research studies, there are more reports of allergies to rodents than other laboratory animals. Most workers who develop allergies to laboratory animals will do so within the first twelve months of working with them. Sometimes reactions only occur in workers after they have been handling animals for several years. Initially, the symptoms are present within minutes of the worker's exposure to the animals. Approximately half of allergic workers will have their initial symptoms subside and then recur three or four hours following the exposure.

Employers should adopt the following best practices to reduce allergic responses of workers:
- Eliminate or minimize exposure to the proteins found in animal urine, saliva and dander.
- Limit the chances that workers will inhale or have skin contact with animal proteins by using well-designed air handling and waste management systems.
- Have workers use appropriate PPE (e.g., gloves, gowns, hair covers, respirators) to further minimize their risk of exposure.

Zoonotic Diseases

There are a host of possible infectious agents that can be transferred from animals to humans. These are referred to as zoonotic diseases. The common routes of exposure to infectious agents are inhalation, inoculation, ingestion and contamination of skin and mucous membranes. Inhalation hazards may arise during work practices that can generate aerosols. These include the following: centrifugation, mixing (e.g., blending, vortexing, and sonication), pouring/decanting and spilling/splashing of culture fluids. Inoculation hazards include needlesticks and lacerations from sharp objects. Ingestion hazards include the following: splashes to the mouth, placing contaminated articles/fingers in mouth, consumption of food in the laboratory, and mouth pipetting. Contamination of skin and mucous membranes can occur via splashes or contact with contaminated fomites (e.g., towels, bedclothes, cups, money). Some of the zoonotic diseases that can be acquired from animals are listed below.

Zoonotic Diseases – Wild and Domesticated Animals

Wild rodents and other wild animals may inflict an injury such as a bite or scratch. Workers need to receive training on the correct way to capture and handle any wild animals. While they may carry or shed organisms that may be potentially infectious to humans, the primary health risk to individuals working with captured animals is the development of an allergy. The development of disease in the human host often requires a preexisting state that compromises the immune system. Workers who have an immune compromising medical condition or who are taking medications that impair the immune system (steroids, immunosuppressive drugs, or chemotherapy) are at higher risk for contracting a rodent disease.

Wild rodents may act as carriers for viruses such as Hantavirus and lymphocytic choriomeningitis virus (LCMV) depending on where they were captured. Additionally, each rodent species may harbor their own range of bacterial diseases, such as tularemia and plague. These animals may also have biting insect vectors which can act as a potential carrier of disease (mouse to human transmission).

Examples of zoonotic diseases that can be transmitted from wild and domesticated animals to humans are listed in the table at page 45 in the Appendix.

Zoonotic Diseases – Non-human Primates (e.g., monkeys)

It should not be surprising that, given our many similarities, humans and non-human primates are susceptible to similar infectious agents. Because of our differences, the consequences of infection with the same agent often vary considerably. Infection may cause few if any symptoms in one group and may be lethal to the other. Exposures to body fluids from non-human primates should be treated immediately.

In 2003, a report entitled, *Occupational Safety and Health in the Care and Use of Non-Human Primates* (see References) was published. This report covers topics relevant to facilities in which non-human primates are housed or where non-human primate blood or tissues are handled. The report describes the hazards associated with work involving non-human primates and discusses the components of a successful occupational health and safety program, including hazard identification, risk assessment and management, institutional management of workers after a suspected occupational exposure, applicable safety regulations, and personnel training.

Employers should ensure that workers are trained to adhere to the following good practices to prevent exposure to zoonotic diseases when working with research animals:

- Avoid use of sharps whenever possible. Take extreme care when using a needle and syringe to inject research animals or when using sharps during necropsy procedures. Never remove, recap, bend, break, or clip used needles from disposable syringes. Use safety engineered needles when practical.
- Take extra precautions when handling hoofed animals. Due to the physical hazards of weight and strength of the animal, large hoofed mammals pose additional concerns for workers. Hoofed mammals may resist handling and may require multiple workers to administer medication or perform other functions.
- Keep hands away from mouth, nose and eyes.
- Wear appropriate PPE (i.e., gloves, gowns, face protection) in all areas within the animal facility.
  - A safety specialist may recommend additional precautions, based upon a risk assessment of the work performed.
- Wear tear-resistant gloves to prevent exposure by animal bites. Micro-tears in the gloves may compromise the protection they offer.
- Remove gloves and wash hands after handling animals or tissues derived from them and before leaving areas where animals are kept.
- Use mechanical pipetting devices (no mouth pipetting).
- Never eat, drink, smoke, handle contact lenses, apply cosmetics, or take or apply medicine in areas where research animals are kept.
- Perform procedures carefully to reduce the possibility of creating splashes or aerosols.
- Contain operations that generate hazardous aerosols in BSCs or other ventilated enclosures, such as animal bedding dump stations.
- Wear eye protection.
- Wear head/hair covering to protect against sprays or splashes of potentially infectious fluids.
- Keep doors closed to rooms where research animals are kept.
- Clean all spills immediately.
- Report all incidents and equipment malfunctions to the supervisor.
- Promptly decontaminate work surfaces when procedures are completed and after surfaces are soiled by spills of animal material or waste.
- Properly dispose of animal waste and bedding.
- Workers should report all work-related injuries and illnesses to their supervisor immediately.
- Following a bite by an animal or other injury in which the wound may be contaminated, first aid should be initiated at the work site.

- Contaminated skin and wounds should be washed thoroughly with soap and water for 15 minutes.
  - Contaminated eyes and mucous membranes should be irrigated for 15 minutes using normal saline or water.
- Consult an occupational health physician concerning wound care standard operating procedures (SOPs) for particular animal bites/scratches.

> An OSHA QuickCard™ entitled **Laboratory Safety – Working with Small Animals** has been developed to supplement this section and is available online at www.osha.gov.

Specific Engineering Control – Biological Safety Cabinets (BSCs)

Properly maintained BSCs, when used in conjunction with good microbiological techniques, provide an effective containment system for safe manipulation of moderate and high-risk infectious agents [Biosafety Level 2 (BSL 2) and 3 (BSL 3) agents]. BSCs protect laboratory workers and the immediate environment from infectious aerosols generated within the cabinet.

Biosafety Cabinet Certifications

BSCs must be certified when installed, whenever they are moved and at least annually, 29 CFR 1030(e)(2)(iii)(B).

> An OSHA Fact Sheet entitled **Laboratory Safety – Biosafety Cabinets (BSCs)** has been developed to supplement this section and is available online at www.osha.gov.

Physical Hazards and Others

Besides exposure to chemicals and biological agents, laboratory workers can also be exposed to a number of physical hazards. Some of the common physical hazards that they may encounter include the following: ergonomic, ionizing radiation, non-ionizing radiation and noise hazards. These hazards are described below in individual sections.

Ergonomic Hazards

Laboratory workers are at risk for repetitive motion injuries during routine laboratory procedures such as pipetting, working at microscopes, operating microtomes, using cell counters and keyboarding at computer workstations. Repetitive motion injuries develop over time and occur when muscles and joints are stressed, tendons are inflamed, nerves are pinched and the flow of blood is restricted. Standing and working in awkward positions in front of laboratory hoods/biological safety cabinets can also present ergonomic problems.

By becoming familiar with how to control laboratory ergonomics-related risk factors, employers can reduce chances for occupational injuries while improving worker comfort, productivity, and job satisfaction. In addition to the general ergonomic guidance, laboratory employers are reminded of some simple adjustments that can be made at the workplace. While there is currently no specific OSHA standard relating to ergonomics in the laboratory workplace, it is recommended that employers provide the information to laboratory workers contained in the new OSHA fact sheet highlighted below.

> An OSHA Fact Sheet entitled **Laboratory Safety – Ergonomics for the Prevention of Musculoskeletal Disorders in Laboratories** has been developed to supplement this section and is available online at osha.gov.

Ionizing Radiation

OSHA's Ionizing Radiation standard, 29 CFR 1910.1096, sets forth the limitations on exposure to radiation from atomic particles. Ionizing radiation sources are found in a wide range of occupational settings, including laboratories. These radiation sources can pose a considerable health risk to affected workers if not properly controlled.

Any laboratory possessing or using radioactive isotopes must be licensed by the Nuclear Regulatory Commission (NRC) and/or by a state agency that has been approved by the NRC, 10 CFR 31.11 and 10 CFR 35.12.

The fundamental objectives of radiation protection measures are: (1) to limit entry of radionuclides into the human body (via ingestion, inhalation, absorption, or through open wounds) to quantities as low as reasonably achievable (ALARA) and always within the established limits; and (2) to limit exposure to external radiation to levels that are within established dose limits and as far below these limits as is reasonably achievable.

All areas in which radioactive materials are used or stored must conspicuously display the symbol for radiation hazards and access should be restricted to authorized personnel.

RADIATION

The OSHA Ionizing Radiation standard requires precautionary measures and personnel monitoring for workers who are likely to be exposed to radiation hazards. Personnel monitoring devices (film badges, thermoluminescent dosimeters (TLD), pocket dosimeters, etc.) must be supplied and used if required to measure an individual's radiation exposure from gamma, neutron, energetic beta, and X-ray sources. The standard monitoring device is a clip-on badge or ring badge bearing the individual assignee's name, date of the monitoring period and a unique identification number. The badges are provided, processed and reported through a commercial service company that meets current requirements of the National Institute of Standards and Technology's National Voluntary Laboratory Accreditation Program (NIST NVLAP).

It is important for employers to understand and follow all applicable regulations for the use of isotopes. In institutional settings, it is the responsibility of each institution to ensure compliance with local, state, and federal laws and regulations; to obtain licenses for official use of radioactive substances; and to designate a radiation safety officer (RSO) to oversee and ensure compliance with state and/or NRC requirements. Information on radioactive materials licenses may be obtained from the Department of Public Health from individual states or from the NRC.

The following OSHA Safety and Health Topics Page provides links to technical and regulatory information on the control of occupational hazards from ionizing radiation: www.osha.gov/SLTC/radiationionizing/index.html.

Non-ionizing Radiation

Non-ionizing radiation is described as a series of energy waves composed of oscillating electric and magnetic fields traveling at the speed of light. Non-ionizing radiation includes the spectrum of ultraviolet (UV), visible light, infrared (IR), microwave (MW), radio frequency (RF), and extremely low frequency (ELF). Lasers commonly operate in the UV, visible, and IR frequencies. Non-ionizing radiation is found in a wide range of occupational settings and can pose a considerable health risk to potentially exposed workers if not properly controlled.

The following OSHA Safety and Health Topics Pages provide links to technical and regulatory information on the control of occupational hazards from non-ionizing radiation and are available at: www.osha.gov/SLTC/radiation_nonionizing/index.html.

Extremely Low Frequency Radiation (ELF)
Extremely Low Frequency (ELF) radiation at 60 HZ is produced by power lines, electrical wiring, and electrical equipment. Common sources of intense exposure include ELF induction furnaces and high-voltage power lines.

Radiofrequency and Microwave Radiation
Microwave radiation (MW) is absorbed near the skin, while radiofrequency (RF) radiation may be absorbed throughout the body. At high enough intensities both will damage tissue through heating. Sources of RF and MW radiation include radio emitters and cell phones.

Infrared Radiation (IR)
The skin and eyes absorb infrared radiation (IR) as heat. Workers normally notice excessive exposure through heat sensation and pain. Sources of IR radiation include heat lamps and IR lasers.

Visible Light Radiation
The different visible frequencies of the electromagnetic (EM) spectrum are "seen" by our eyes as different colors. Good lighting is conducive to increased production, and may help prevent incidents related to poor lighting conditions. Excessive visible radiation can damage the eyes and skin.

Ultraviolet Radiation (UV)
Ultraviolet radiation (UV) has a high photon energy range and is particularly hazardous because there are usually no immediate symptoms of excessive exposure. Sources of UV radiation in the laboratory include black lights and UV lasers.

Laser Hazards
Lasers typically emit optical (UV, visible light, IR) radiations and are primarily an eye and skin hazard. Common lasers include CO_2 IR laser; helium - neon, neodymium YAG, and ruby visible lasers, and the Nitrogen UV laser.

LASER is an acronym which stands for Light Amplification by Stimulated Emission of Radiation.

The laser produces an intense, highly directional beam of light. The most common cause of laser-induced tissue damage is thermal in nature, where the tissue proteins are denatured due to the temperature rise following absorption of laser energy.

The human body is vulnerable to the output of certain lasers, and under certain circumstances, exposure can result in damage to the eye and skin. Research relating to injury thresholds of the eye and skin has been carried out in order to understand the biological hazards of laser radiation. It is now widely accepted that the human eye is almost always more vulnerable to injury than human skin.

Noise

OSHA's Occupational Noise Exposure standard, 29 CFR 1910.95, requires employers to develop and implement a hearing conservation program that includes the use of PPE (e.g., hearing protectors), if workers are exposed to a time-weighted average (TWA) of ≥ 85 dBA over an 8-hour work shift. In addition, when workers are exposed to noise levels ≥ 85 dBA, the employer must develop a monitoring program to assess noise levels. The monitoring program must include the following components:

- All continuous, intermittent, and impulsive sound levels from 80-130 dBA must be included in noise measurements, 29 CFR 1910.95(d)(2)(i);
- Instruments used to measure worker noise exposure must be calibrated to ensure measurement accuracy, 29 CFR 1910.95(d)(2)(ii); and
- Monitoring must be repeated whenever a change in production, process, equipment, or controls increases noise exposures, 29 CFR 1910.95(d)(3).

Laboratory workers are exposed to noise from a variety of sources. Operation of large analyzers (e.g., chemistry analyzer), fume hoods, biological safety cabinets, incubators, centrifuges (especially ultracentrifuges), cell washers, sonicators, and stirrer motors, all contribute to the noise level in laboratories. Further sources of noise in laboratories include fans and compressors for cryostats, refrigerators, refrigerated centrifuges, and freezers. As an example, a high-speed refrigerated centrifuge alone can generate noise levels as high as 65 dBA. To provide some further context, a whisper registers approximately 30 dBA; normal conversation about 50 to 60 dBA; a ringing phone 80 dBA and a power mower 90 dBA. If noise levels exceed 80 dBA, people must speak very loudly to be heard, while at noise levels of 85 to 90 dBA, people have to shout.

In order to determine if the noise levels in the laboratory are above the threshold level that damages hearing, the employer must conduct a noise exposure assessment using an approved sound level monitoring device, such as a dosimeter, and measuring an 8-hour TWA exposure. If the noise levels are found to exceed the threshold level, the employer must provide hearing protection at no cost to the workers and train them in the proper use of the protectors. The potential dangers of miscommunicating instructions or laboratory results are obvious, and efforts should be made to improve the design of clinical laboratories and to evaluate new instrumentation with regard to the impact of these factors on worker noise exposure. The employer should evaluate the possibility of relocating equipment to another area or using engineering controls to reduce the noise level below an 8-hour TWA of 85 dBA in order to comply with OSHA's Occupational Noise Exposure standard.

While most laboratories' noise levels do not equal or exceed the 8-hour TWA of 85 dBA, certain accrediting agencies are implementing special emphasis programs on noise reduction in the laboratory. Because noise is becoming more of a concern in the clinical setting, the College of American Pathologists has added evaluation of noise in the laboratory under their general checklist for accreditation (GEN.70824).

Health Effects

Exposure to continuous noise may lead to the following stress-related symptoms:
- Depression;
- Irritability;
- Decreased concentration in the workplace;
- Reduced efficiency and decreased productivity;
- Noise-induced hearing loss;
- Tinnitus (i.e., ringing in the ears); and
- Increased errors in laboratory work.

There are several steps that employers can take to minimize the noise in the laboratory, including:
- Moving noise-producing equipment (e.g., freezers, refrigerators, incubators and centrifuges) from the laboratory to an equipment room;
- Locating compressors for controlled-temperature rooms remotely; and
- Providing acoustical treatment on ceilings and walls.

Safety Hazards

Employers must assess tasks to identify potential worksite hazards and provide and ensure that workers use appropriate personal protective equipment (PPE) as stated in the PPE standard, 29 CFR 1910.132.

Employers must require workers to use appropriate hand protection when hands are exposed to hazards such as sharp instruments and potential thermal burns. Examples of PPE which may be selected include using oven mitts when handling hot items, and steel mesh or cut-resistant gloves when handling or sorting sharp instruments as stated in the Hand Protection standard, 29 CFR 1910.138.

Autoclaves and Sterilizers

Workers should be trained to recognize the potential for exposure to burns or cuts that can occur from handling or sorting hot sterilized items or sharp instruments when removing them from autoclaves/sterilizers or from steam lines that service the autoclaves.

In order to prevent injuries from occurring, employers must train workers to follow good work practices such as those outlined in the QuickCard™ highlighted below.

Centrifuges

Centrifuges, due to the high speed at which they operate, have great potential for injuring users if not operated properly. Unbalanced centrifuge rotors can result in injury, even death. Sample container breakage can generate aerosols that may be harmful if inhaled.

The majority of all centrifuge accidents are the result of user error. In order to prevent injuries or exposure to dangerous substances, employers should train workers to follow good work practices such as those outlined in the QuickCard™ highlighted below.

Employers should instruct workers when centrifuging infectious materials that they should wait 10 minutes after the centrifuge rotor has stopped before opening the lid. Workers should also be trained to use appropriate decontamination and cleanup procedures for the materials being centrifuged if a spill occurs and to report all accidents to their supervisor immediately.

Compressed Gases

According to OSHA's Laboratory standard, a "**compressed gas**" (1) is a gas or mixture of gases in a container having an absolute pressure exceeding 40 pounds per square inch (psi) at 70°F (21.1°C); or (2) is a gas or mixture of gases having an absolute pressure exceeding 104 psi at 130°F (54.4°C) regardless of the pressure at 70°F (21.1°C); or (3) is a liquid having a vapor pressure exceeding 40 psi at 100°F (37.8°C) as determined by ASTM (American Society for Testing and Materials) D-323-72, [29 CFR 1910.1450(c)(1)-(3)].

Within laboratories, compressed gases are usually supplied either through fixed piped gas systems or individual cylinders of gases. Compressed gases can be toxic, flammable, oxidizing, corrosive, or inert. Leakage of any of these gases can be hazardous. Leaking inert gases (e.g., nitrogen) can quickly displace air in a large area creating an oxygen-deficient atmosphere; toxic gases (e.g., can create poison atmospheres; and flammable (oxygen) or reactive gases can result in fire and exploding cylinders. In addition, there are hazards from the pressure of the gas and the physical weight of the cylinder. A gas cylinder falling over can break containers and crush feet. The gas cylinder can itself become a missile if the cylinder valve is broken off. Laboratories must include compressed gases in their inventory of chemicals in their Chemical Hygiene Plan.

Compressed gases contained in cylinders vary in chemical properties, ranging from inert and harmless to toxic and explosive. The high pressure of the gases constitutes a serious hazard in the event that gas cylinders sustain physical damage and/or are exposed to high temperatures.

Store, handle, and use compressed gases in accord with OSHA's Compressed Gases standard (29 CFR 1910.101) and Pamphlet P-1-1965 from the Compressed Gas Association.

- All cylinders whether empty or full must be stored upright.
- Secure cylinders of compressed gases. Cylinders should never be dropped or allowed to strike each other with force.
- Transport compressed gas cylinders with protective caps in place and do not roll or drag the cylinders.

Cryogens and Dry Ice

Cryogens, substances used to produce very low temperatures [below -153°C (-243°F)], such as liquid nitrogen (LN_2) which has a boiling point of -196°C (-321°F), are commonly used in laboratories. Although not a cryogen, solid carbon dioxide or dry ice which converts directly to carbon dioxide gas at -78°C (-109°F) is also often used in laboratories. Shipments packed with dry ice, samples preserved with liquid nitrogen, and in some cases, techniques that use cryogenic liquids, such as cryogenic grinding of samples, present potential hazards in the laboratory.

Overview of Cryogenic Safety Hazards

The safety hazards associated with the use of cryogenic liquids are categorized as follows:

(1) *Cold contact burns*
Liquid or low-temperature gas from any cryogenic substance will produce effects on the skin similar to a burn.

(2) *Asphyxiation*
Degrees of asphyxia will occur when the oxygen content of the working environment is less than 20.9% by volume. This decrease in oxygen content can be caused by a failure/leak of a cryogenic vessel or transfer line and subsequent vaporization of the cryogen. Effects from oxygen deficiency become noticeable at levels below approximately 18% and sudden death may occur at approximately 6% oxygen content by volume.

(3) *Explosion - Pressure*
Heat flux into the cryogen from the environment will vaporize the liquid and potentially cause pressure buildup in cryogenic containment vessels and transfer lines. Adequate pressure relief should be provided to all parts of a system to permit this routine outgassing and prevent explosion.

(4) *Explosion - Chemical*
Cryogenic fluids with a boiling point below that of liquid oxygen are able to condense oxygen from the atmosphere. Repeated replenishment of the system can thereby cause oxygen to accumulate as an unwanted contaminant. Similar oxygen enrichment may occur where condensed air accumulates on the exterior of cryogenic piping. Violent reactions, e.g., rapid combustion or explosion, may occur if the materials which make contact with the oxygen are combustible.

Employer Responsibility

It is the responsibility of the employer, specifically the supervisor in charge of an apparatus, to ensure that the cryogenic safety hazards are minimized. This will entail (1) a safety analysis and review for all cryogenic facilities, (2) cryogenic safety and operational training for relevant workers, (3) appropriate maintenance of cryogenic systems in their original working order, i.e., the condition in which the system was approved for use, and (4) upkeep of inspection schedules and records.

Employers must train workers to use the appropriate personal protective equipment (PPE)

Whenever handling or transfer of cryogenic fluids might result in exposure to the cold liquid, boil-off gas, or surface, protective clothing must be worn. This includes:

- face shield or safety goggles;
- safety gloves; and
- long-sleeved shirts, lab coats, aprons.

Eye protection is required at all times when working with cryogenic fluids. When pouring a cryogen, working with a wide-mouth Dewar flask or around the exhaust of cold boil-off gas, use of a full face shield is recommended.

Hand protection is required to guard against the hazard of touching cold surfaces. It is recommended that Cryogen Safety Gloves be used by the worker.

> An OSHA QuickFacts entitled **Laboratory Safety – Cryogens and Dry Ice** has been developed to supplement this section and is available online at www.osha.gov.

Electrical

In the laboratory, there is the potential for workers to be exposed to electrical hazards including electric shock, electrocutions, fires and explosions. Damaged electrical cords can lead to possible shocks or electrocutions. A flexible electrical cord may be damaged by door or window edges, by staples and fastenings, by equipment rolling over it, or simply by aging.

The potential for possible electrocution or electric shock or contact with electrical hazards can result from a number of factors, including the following:
- Faulty electrical equipment/instrumentation or wiring;
- Damaged receptacles and connectors; and
- Unsafe work practices.

Employers are responsible for complying with OSHA's standard 1910 Subpart S-Electrical

Subpart S is comprehensive and addresses electrical safety requirements for the practical safeguarding of workers in their workplaces. This Subpart includes, but is not limited to, these requirements:
- Electrical equipment must be free from recognized hazards, 29 CFR 1910.303(b)(1);
- Listed or labeled equipment must be used or installed in accord with any instructions included in the listing or labeling, 29 CFR 1910.303(b)(2);
- Sufficient access and working space must be provided and maintained around all electrical equipment operating at ≤ 600 volts to permit ready and safe operation and maintenance of such equipment, 29 CFR 1910.303(g)(1);
- Ensure that all electrical service near sources of water is properly grounded.
- Tag out and remove from service all damaged receptacles and portable electrical equipment, 29 CFR 1910.334(a)(2)(ii);
- Repair all damaged receptacles and portable electrical equipment before placing them back into service, 29 CFR 1910.334(a)(2)(ii);
- Ensure that workers are trained not to plug or unplug energized equipment when their hands are wet, 29 CFR 1910.334(a)(5)(i);
- Select and use appropriate work practices, 29 CFR 1910.333; and
- Follow requirements for Hazardous Classified Locations, 29 CFR 1910.307. This section covers the requirements for electric equipment and wiring in locations that are classified based on the properties of the flammable vapors, liquids or gases, or combustible dusts or fibers that may be present therein and the likelihood that a flammable or combustible concentration or quantity is present.

Notes:
- Only "Qualified Persons," as defined by OSHA in 29 CFR 1910.399, are to work on electrical circuits/systems.
- Workers must be trained to know the locations of circuit breaker panels that serve their lab area.

An OSHA QuickFacts entitled **Laboratory Safety – Electrical Hazards** has been developed to supplement this section and is available online at www.osha.gov.

Fire

Fire is the most common serious hazard that one faces in a typical laboratory. While proper procedures and training can minimize the chances of an accidental fire, laboratory workers should still be prepared to deal with a fire emergency should it occur. In dealing with a laboratory fire, all containers of infectious materials should be placed into autoclaves, incubators, refrigerators, or freezers for containment.

Small bench-top fires in laboratory spaces are not uncommon. Large laboratory fires are rare. However, the risk of severe injury or death is significant because fuel load and hazard levels in labs are typically very high. Laboratories, especially those using solvents in any quantity, have the potential for flash fires, explosion, rapid spread of fire, and high toxicity of products of combustion (heat, smoke, and flame).

Employers should ensure that workers are trained to do the following in order to prevent fires

- Plan work. Have a written emergency plan for your space and/or operation.
- Minimize materials. Have present in the immediate work area and use only the minimum quantities necessary for work in progress. Not only does this minimize fire risk, it reduces costs and waste.
- Observe proper housekeeping. Keep work areas uncluttered, and clean frequently. Put unneeded materials back in storage promptly. Keep aisles, doors, and access to emergency equipment unobstructed at all times.
- Observe restrictions on equipment (i.e., keeping solvents only in an explosion-proof refrigerator).
- Keep barriers in place (shields, hood doors, lab doors).

OSHA®
Occupational Safety and
Health Administration

- Wear proper clothing and personal protective equipment.
- Avoid working alone.
- Store solvents properly in approved flammable liquid storage cabinets.
- Shut door behind you when evacuating.
- Limit open flames use to under fume hoods and only when constantly attended.
- Keep combustibles away from open flames.
- Do not heat solvents using hot plates.
- Remember the "RACE" rule in case of a fire.
  - R= Rescue/remove all occupants
  - A= Activate the alarm system
  - C= Confine the fire by closing doors
  - E= Evacuate/Extinguish

Employers should ensure that workers are trained in the following emergency procedures
- Know what to do. You tend to do under stress what you have practiced or pre-planned. Therefore, planning, practice and drills are essential.
- Know where things are: The nearest fire extinguisher, fire alarm box, exit(s), telephone, emergency shower/eyewash, and first-aid kit, etc.
- Be aware that emergencies are rarely "clean" and will often involve more than one type of problem. For example, an explosion may generate medical, fire, and contamination emergencies simultaneously.
- Train workers and exercise the emergency plan.
- Learn to use the emergency equipment provided.

Employers must be knowledgeable about OSHA's Portable Fire Extinguishers standard, 29 CFR 1910.157, and train workers to be aware of the different fire extinguisher types and how to use them. OSHA's Portable Fire Extinguishers standard, 29 CFR 1910.157, applies to the placement, use, maintenance, and testing of portable fire extinguishers provided for the use of workers. This standard requires that a fire extinguisher be placed within 75 feet for Class A fire risk (ordinary combustibles; usually fuels that burn and leave "ash") and within 50 feet for high-risk Class B fire risk (flammable liquids and gases; in the laboratory many organic solvents and compressed gases are fire hazards).

The two most common types of extinguishers in the chemistry laboratory are pressurized dry chemical (Type BC or ABC) and carbon dioxide. In addition, you may also have a specialized Class D dry powder extinguisher for use on flammable metal fires. Water-filled extinguishers are not acceptable for laboratory use.

Employers should train workers to remember the "PASS" rule for fire extinguishers
PASS summarizes the operation of a fire extinguisher.
P – Pull the pin
A – Aim extinguisher nozzle at the base of the fire
S – Squeeze the trigger while holding the extinguisher upright
S – Sweep the extinguisher from side to side; cover the fire with the spray

Employers should train workers on appropriate procedures in the event of a clothing fire
- If the floor is not on fire, STOP, DROP and ROLL to extinguish the flames or use a fire blanket or a safety shower if not contraindicated (i.e., there are no chemicals or electricity involved).
- If a coworker's clothing catches fire and he/she runs down the hallway in panic, tackle him/her and smother the flames as quickly as possible, using appropriate means that are available (e.g., fire blanket, fire extinguisher).

Lockout/Tagout
Workers performing service or maintenance on equipment may be exposed to injuries from the unexpected energization, startup of the equipment, or release or stored energy in the equipment. OSHA's Control of Hazardous Energy standard, 29 CFR 1910.147, commonly referred to as the "Lockout/Tagout" standard, requires the adoption and implementation of practices and procedures to shut down equipment, isolate it from its energy source(s), and prevent the release of potentially hazardous energy while maintenance and servicing activities are being performed. It contains minimum performance requirements, and definitive criteria for establishing an effective program for the control of hazardous energy. However, employers have the flexibility to develop Lockout/Tagout programs that are suitable for their respective facilities.

This standard establishes basic requirements involved in locking and/or tagging equipment while installation, maintenance, testing, repair or construction operations are in progress. The primary purpose is to prevent hazardous exposure to personnel and possible equipment damage. The procedures apply to the shutdown of all potential energy sources associated with the equipment. These could include pressures, flows of fluids and gases, electrical power, and radiation. This standard covers the servicing and maintenance of machines and equipment in which the "**unexpected**" energization or startup of the machines or equipment, or release of stored energy could cause injury to workers.

Under the standard, the term "unexpected" also covers situations in which the servicing and/or maintenance is performed during ongoing normal production operations if:
- A worker is required to remove or bypass machine guards or other safety devices, 29 CFR 1910.147(a)2)(ii)(A) or
- A worker is required to place any part of his or her body into a point of operation or into an area on a machine or piece of equipment where work is performed, or into the danger zone associated with the machine's operation, 29 CFR 1910.147(a)(2)(ii)(B).

The Lockout/Tagout standard establishes minimum performance requirements for the control of such hazardous energy.

Maintenance activities can be performed with or without energy present. A probable, underlying cause of many accidents resulting in injury during maintenance is that work is performed without the knowledge that the system, whether energized or not, can produce hazardous energy. Unexpected and unrestricted release of hazardous energy can occur if: (1) all energy sources are not identified; (2) provisions are not made for safe work practices with energy present; or (3) deactivated energy sources are reactivated, mistakenly, intentionally, or accidentally, without the maintenance worker's knowledge.

Problems involving control of hazardous energy require procedural solutions. Employers must adopt such procedural solutions for controlling hazards to ensure worker safety during maintenance. However, such procedures are effective only if strictly enforced. Employers must, therefore, be committed to strict implementation of such procedures.

Trips, Slips and Falls

Worker exposure to wet floors or spills and clutter can lead to slips/trips/falls and other possible injuries. In order to keep workers safe, employers are referred to OSHA standard 29 CFR 1910 Subpart D – Walking-Working Surfaces, Subpart E - Means of Egress, and Subpart J - General environmental controls which states the following:

- Keep floors clean and dry, 29 CFR 1910.22(a)(2). In addition to being a slip hazard, continually wet surfaces promote the growth of mold, fungi, and bacteria that can cause infections.
- Provide warning (caution) signs for wet floor areas, 29 CFR 1910.145(c)(2).
- Where wet processes are used, maintain drainage and provide false floors, platforms, mats, or other dry standing places where practicable, or provide appropriate waterproof footgear, 29 CFR 1910.141(a)(3)(ii).
- The Walking/Working Surfaces standard requires that all employers keep all places of employment clean and orderly and in a sanitary condition, 29 CFR 1910.22(a)(1).
- Keep aisles and passageways clear and in good repair, with no obstruction across or in aisles that could create a hazard, 29 CFR 1910.22(b)(1). Provide floor plugs for equipment, so that power cords need not run across pathways.
- Keep exits free from obstruction. Access to exits must remain clear of obstructions at all times, 29 CFR 1910.37(a)(3).
- Ensure that spills are reported and cleaned up immediately.
- Eliminate cluttered or obstructed work areas.
- Use prudent housekeeping procedures such as using caution signs, cleaning only one side of a passageway at a time, and provide good lighting for all halls and stairwells to help reduce accidents, especially during the night hours.
- Instruct workers to use the handrail on stairs, to avoid undue speed, and to maintain an unobstructed view of the stairs ahead of them even if that means requesting help to manage a bulky load.
- Eliminate uneven floor surfaces.
- Promote safe work practices, even in cramped working spaces.
- Avoid awkward positions, and use equipment that makes lifting easier.

References

American Chemical Society, Safety in Academic Chemistry Laboratories. 1990. 5th Edition.

Burnett L, Lunn G, Coico R. Biosafety: Guidelines for working with pathogenic and infectious microorganisms. Current Protocols in Microbiology. 2009. 13:1A.1.1.-1A.1.14.

Centers for Disease Control and Prevention (CDC), National Institutes of Health (NIH). Primary Containment for Biohazards: Selection, Installation, and Use of Biological Safety Cabinets. 2007. 3rd Edition.

Centers for Disease Control and Prevention (CDC), National Institutes of Health (NIH). Biosafety Manual. 2007. 5th Edition. Washington, DC: U.S. Government Printing Office.

Centers for Disease Control and Prevention (CDC), Safety Survival Skills II. Laboratory Safety. A Primer on Safe Laboratory Practice and Emergency Response for CDC Workers. 2004. Available at: www.cdc.gov/od/ohs/safety/S2.pdf (Accessed January 7, 2009).

Clinical Laboratory Standards Institute (formerly NCCLS) document GP17-A2. Clinical Laboratory Safety. 2nd Edition. 2004.

Clinical Laboratory Standards Institute (formerly NCCLS) document GP18-A2. Laboratory Design. 2nd Edition. 2007.

Clinical Laboratory Standards Institute (formerly NCCLS) document M29-A3. Protection of Laboratory Workers from Occupationally Acquired Infections. 3rd Edition. 2005.

Committee on Occupational Health and Safety in the Care and Use of Non-human Primates, National Research Council. 2003. Occupational Health and Safety in the Care and Use of Non-human Primates. 2003. The National Academy Press, Washington, D.C.

Darragh AR, Harrison H, Kenny S. Effect of ergonomics intervention on workstations of microscope workers. American Journal of Occupational Therapy. 2008. 62:61-69.

Davis D. Laboratory Safety: A Self Assessment Workbook, ASCP Press, 1st Edition, 2008.

Furr AK. CRC Handbook of Laboratory Safety, 5th Edition, Chemical Rubber Company Press, 2000.

Gile TJ. Ergonomics in the laboratory. Lab Med. 2001. 32:263-267.

Illinois State University. Chemical Hygiene Plan for Chemistry Laboratories: Information and Training, 1995.

Kimman TG, Smit E, Klein MR. Evidence-based biosafety: A review of the principles and effectiveness of microbiological containment. Clinical Microbiology Reviews. 2008. 21:403-425.

National Institute of Occupational Safety and Health, Registry of Toxic Effects of Chemical Substances, (published annually) U.S. Department of Health and Human Services, Occupational Health Guidelines for Chemical Hazards, NIOSH/OSHA.

National Research Council, Prudent Practices in the Laboratory: Handling and Management of Chemical Hazards, National Academy Press, 2011.

Rose S. Clinical Laboratory Safety. J.B. Lippincott. Philadelphia, PA, 1984.

Singh K. Laboratory-acquired infections. Clinical Infectious Diseases. 2009. 49:142-147.

University of Illinois at Urbana-Champaign. UIUC Model Chemical Hygiene Plan, 1999.

University of Nebraska – Lincoln. UNL Environmental Health and Safety. Safe Operating Procedures, 2005-2008.

Vecchio D, Sasco AJ, Cann CI. 2003. Occupational risk in health care and research. American Journal of Industrial Medicine. 43:369-397.

Appendices

Additional OSHA Information

Chemical Hazards

Laboratory workers may be exposed to a variety of hazardous chemicals on the job. The following OSHA resources provide information on how to prevent or reduce exposure to some of the more common chemicals.

OSHA Standards

The Air Contaminants standard (1910.1000) provides rules for protecting workers from exposure to over 400 chemicals.
- Complete standard
  - **29 CFR 1910.1000**
    http://www.osha.gov/pls/oshaweb/owadisp.show_document?p_table=STANDARDS&p_id=9991
- Hospital eTool
  - *Laboratories – Common safety and health topics*
    - *Toluene, Xylene, or Acrylamide Exposure*
      http://www.osha.gov/SLTC/etools/hospital/lab/lab.html#Toulene,Xylene,orAcrylamideExposure

The Ethylene Oxide standard (29 CFR 1910.1047) requires employers to provide workers with protection from occupational exposure to ethylene oxide (EtO).
- Complete standard
  - **29 CFR 1910.1047**
    http://www.osha.gov/pls/oshaweb/owadisp.show_document?p_table=STANDARDS&p_id=10070
- Fact Sheet
  - *Ethylene Oxide*
    http://www.osha.gov/OshDoc/data_General_Facts/ethylene-oxide-factsheet.pdf
- Booklet
  - *Ethylene Oxide (EtO): Understanding OSHA's Exposure Monitoring Requirements*.
    OSHA Publication 3325 (2007). http://www.osha.gov/Publications/OSHA_ethylene_oxide.pdf
  - *Small Business Guide for Ethylene Oxide*. OSHA Publication 3359 (2009).
    http://www.osha.gov/Publications/ethylene-oxide-final.html
- Safety and Health Topics Page
  - *Ethylene Oxide*
    http://www.osha.gov/SLTC/ethyleneoxide/index.html

The Formaldehyde standard (29 CFR 1910.1048) requires employers to provide workers with protection from occupational exposure to formaldehyde.
- Complete standard
  - **29 CFR 1910.1048**
    http://www.osha.gov/pls/oshaweb/owadisp.show_document?p_table=STANDARDS&p_id=10075
- Fact Sheet
  - *Formaldehyde*
    http://www.osha.gov/OshDoc/data_General_Facts/formaldehyde-factsheet.pdf
- Hospital eTool
  - *Laboratories – Common safety and health topics*
    - *Formaldehyde Exposure*
      http://www.osha.gov/SLTC/etools/hospital/lab/lab.html#FormaldehydeExposure
- Safety and Health Topics Page
  - *Formaldehyde*
    http://www.osha.gov/SLTC/formaldehyde/index.html

The Hazard Communication standard (29 CFR 1910.1200) is designed to protect against chemical source illnesses and injuries by ensuring that employers and employees are provided with sufficient information to recognize, evaluate and control chemical hazards and take appropriate protective measures.

In addition to the information provided at page 13 of this document, the following documents are available in either electronic or hard copy formats or both.

- Complete standard
  - **29 CFR 1910.1200**
    http://www.osha.gov/pls/oshaweb/owadisp.show_document?p_table=STANDARDS&p_id=10099
- Brochures
  - *Chemical Hazard Communication.* OSHA Publication 3084 (1998).
    http://www.osha.gov/Publications/osha3084.pdf
  - *Hazard Communication Guidance for Combustible Dusts.* OSHA Publication 3371 (2009).
    http://www.osha.gov/Publications/osha3371.pdf
  - *Hazard Communication Guidelines for Compliance.* OSHA publication 3111 (2000).
    http://www.osha.gov/Publications/osha3111.pdf
- Sample program
  - *Model Plans and Programs for the OSHA Bloodborne Pathogens and Hazard Communications Standards.* OSHA Publication 3186 (2003).
    http://www.osha.gov/Publications/osha3186.pdf
- QuickFacts
  - *Laboratory Safety – Labeling and Transfer of Chemicals.* OSHA Publication 3410 (2011).
    http://www.osha.gov/Publications/laboratory/OSHAquickfacts-lab-safety-labeling-chemical-transfer.pdf
- Safety and Health Topics Pages
  - *Hazard Communication: Foundation of Workplace Chemical Safety Programs*
    http://www.osha.gov/dsg/hazcom/MSDSenforcementInitiative.html
  - *Hazard Communication – HAZCOM Program*
    http://www.osha.gov/dsg/hazcom/solutions.html
  - *Hazardous Drugs*
    http://www.osha.gov/SLTC/hazardousdrugs/index.html

The Occupational Exposure to Hazardous Chemicals in Laboratories standard (29 CFR 1910.1450), commonly referred to as the Laboratory standard, requires that the employer designate a Chemical Hygiene Officer and have a written Chemical Hygiene Plan (CHP), and actively verify that it remains effective.

In addition to the information provided at page 9 of this document, the following documents are available in either electronic or hard copy formats or both.

- Complete standard
  - **29 CFR 1910.1450**
    http://www.osha.gov/pls/oshaweb/owadisp.show_document?p_table=STANDARDS&p_id=10106
- Fact Sheet
  - *Laboratory Safety – OSHA Laboratory Standard*
    http://www.osha.gov/Publications/laboratory/OSHAfactsheet-laboratory-safety-osha-lab-standard.pdf
  - *Laboratory Safety – Chemical Hygiene Plan*
    http://www.osha.gov/Publications/laboratory/OSHAfactsheet-laboratory-safety-chemical-hygiene-plan.pdf
- Hospital eTool
  http://www.osha.gov/SLTC/etools/hospital/lab/lab.html
  - *Laboratories – Common safety and health topics:*
    - *Bloodborne Pathogens (BBPs)*
      http://www.osha.gov/SLTC/etools/hospital/lab/lab.html#BloodbornePathogens
    - *Tuberculosis (TB)* https://www.osha.gov/SLTC/etools/hospital/lab/lab.html#Tuberculosis
    - *OSHA Laboratory Standard*
      http://www.osha.gov/SLTC/etools/hospital/lab/lab.html#OSHA_Laboratory_Standard
    - *Formaldehyde Exposure*
      http://www.osha.gov/SLTC/etools/hospital/lab/lab.html#FormaldehydeExposure
    - *Toluene, Xylene, or Acrylamide Exposure*
      http://www.osha.gov/SLTC/etools/hospital/lab/lab.html#Toulene,Xylene,orAcrylamideExposure

- ○ **Needle Stick and Sharps Injuries**
  http://www.osha.gov/SLTC/etools/hospital/lab/lab.html#NeedlestickInjuries
- ○ **Work Practices and Behaviors**
  http://www.osha.gov/SLTC/etools/hospital/lab/lab.html#WorkPractices
- ○ **Engineering Controls**
  http://www.osha.gov/SLTC/etools/hospital/lab/lab.html#EngineeringControls
- ○ **Morgue**
  http://www.osha.gov/SLTC/etools/hospital/lab/lab.html#Morgue
- ○ **Latex Allergy**
  http://www.osha.gov/SLTC/etools/hospital/lab/lab.html#LatexAllergy
- ○ **Slips/Trips/Falls**
  http://www.osha.gov/SLTC/etools/hospital/lab/lab.html#Slips/Trips/Falls
- ○ **Ergonomics**
  http://www.osha.gov/SLTC/etools/hospital/lab/lab.html#Ergonomics

Additional OSHA Information on Chemical Hazards

Beryllium
- Hazard Information Bulletin
  - ▪ **Preventing Adverse Effects from Exposure to Beryllium in Dental Laboratories**. (2002).
    http://www.osha.gov/dts/hib/hib_data/hib20020419.html
- Safety and Health Topics Page
  - ▪ **Beryllium**
    http://www.osha.gov/SLTC/beryllium/index.html

Glutaraldehyde
- Booklet
  - ▪ **Best Practices for the Safe Use of Glutaraldehyde in Health Care**. OSHA Publication 3258-08N, (2006).
    http://www.osha.gov/Publications/glutaraldehyde.pdf
- Hospital eTool
  - ▪ **Glutaraldehyde**
    http://www.osha.gov/SLTC/etools/hospital/hazards/glutaraldehyde/glut.html

Latex
- Safety and Health Information Bulletin
  - ▪ **Potential for Sensitization and Possible Allergic Reaction to Natural Rubber Latex Gloves and other Natural Rubber Products**. (2008).
    http://www.osha.gov/dts/shib/shib012808.html
- Letters of Interpretation
  - ▪ **Bloodborne Pathogens and the issue of latex allergy and latex hypersensitivity.** (1995 - 10/23/1995).
    http://www.osha.gov/pls/oshaweb/owadisp.show_document?p_table=INTERPRETATIONS&p_id=21987
  - ▪ **Concern of potential adverse affects from latex by consumers and health care patients with Hevea Natural Rubber Latex Allergy.** (2004 - 01/29/2004).
    http://www.osha.gov/pls/oshaweb/owadisp.show_document?p_table=INTERPRETATIONS&p_id=24742
  - ▪ **Labeling of Latex.** (1996 - 01/11/1996).
    http://www.osha.gov/pls/oshaweb/owadisp.show_document?p_table=INTERPRETATIONS&p_id=22040
- Hospital eTool
  - ▪ **Latex Allergy**
    http://www.osha.gov/SLTC/etools/hospital/hazards/latex/latex.html
- Safety and Health Topics Page
  - ▪ **Latex Allergy**
    http://www.osha.gov/SLTC/latexallergy/index.html
- QuickFacts
  - ▪ **Laboratory Safety - Latex Allergy**. OSHA Publication 3411 (2011).
    http://www.osha.gov/Publications/laboratory/OSHAquickfacts-lab-safety-latex-allergy.pdf

OSHA
Occupational Safety and
Health Administration

Mercury is commonly found in thermometers, manometers, barometers, gauges, valves, switches, batteries, and high-intensity discharge (HID) lamps. It is also used in amalgams for dentistry, preservatives, heat transfer technology, pigments, catalysts, and lubricating oils.

- Safety and Health Topics Page
  - *Mercury*
    http://www.osha.gov/SLTC/mercury/index.html

Biological Hazards

The Bloodborne Pathogens standard (29 CFR 1910.1030), including changes mandated by the *Needlestick Safety and Prevention Act of 2001*, requires employers to protect workers from infection from human bloodborne pathogens in the workplace. The standard covers all workers with "reasonably anticipated" exposure to blood or other potentially infectious materials (OPIM).

- Complete standard
  - **29 CFR 1910.1030**
    http://www.osha.gov/pls/oshaweb/owadisp.show_document?p_table=STANDARDS&p_id=10051
- Standard interpretations
  - *OSHA's standard interpretations for 29 CFR 1910.1030*
    http://www.osha.gov/pls/oshaweb/owasrch.search_form?p_doc_type=INTERPRETATIONS&p_toc_level=3&p_keyvalue=1910.1030&p_status=CURRENT
- Brochure/Sample program
  - *Model Plans and Programs for the OSHA Bloodborne Pathogens and Hazard Communications Standards.* OSHA Publication 3186 (2003).
    http://www.osha.gov/Publications/osha3186.html
- Fact Sheets (Accessible through the Safety and Health Topics Page entitled, *Bloodborne Pathogens and Needlestick Prevention*) NOTE: The links provided below are for the old Fact Sheets. All of these have been updated and approved for publication (2010) - please upload the new Fact Sheets
  - *OSHA's Bloodborne Pathogens Standard*
    http://www.osha.gov/OshDoc/data_BloodborneFacts/bbfact01.pdf
  - *Protecting Yourself When Handling Contaminated Sharps*
    http://www.osha.gov/OshDoc/data_BloodborneFacts/bbfact02.pdf
  - *Personal Protective Equipment Reduces Exposure to Bloodborne Pathogens*
    http://www.osha.gov/OshDoc/data_BloodborneFacts/bbfact03.pdf
  - *Exposure Incidents*
    http://www.osha.gov/OshDoc/data_BloodborneFacts/bbfact04.pdf
  - *Hepatitis B Vaccination Protection*
    http://www.osha.gov/OshDoc/data_BloodborneFacts/bbfact05.pdf
- Safety and Health Topics Page
  - *Bloodborne Pathogens and Needlestick Prevention*
    http://www.osha.gov/SLTC/bloodbornepathogens/index.html
- Safety and Health Information Bulletins
  - *Use of Blunt-Tip Suture Needles to Decrease Percutaneous Injuries to Surgical Personnel.* (2007).
    http://www.cdc.gov/niosh/docs/2008-101/
  - *Disposal of Contaminated Needles and Blood Tube Holders Used for Phlebotomy.* (2003).
    http://www.osha.gov/dts/shib/shib101503.html
  - *Potential for Occupational Exposure to Bloodborne Pathogens from Cleaning Needles Used in Allergy Testing Procedures.* (1995).
    http://www.osha.gov/dts/hib/hib_data/hib19950921.html
  - *Sharps Disposal Containers with Needle Removal Features.* (1993).
    http://www.osha.gov/dts/hib/hib_data/hib19930312.html
- Hospital eTool
  - *Bloodborne Pathogens*
    http://www.osha.gov/SLTC/etools/hospital/hazards/bbp/bbp.html

Additional OSHA Information on Biological Agents

Tuberculosis

- Hospital eTool
  - *Sample Tuberculosis Exposure Control Plan*
    http://www.osha.gov/SLTC/etools/hospital/hazards/tb/sampleexposurecontrolplan.html
  - *Tuberculosis*
    http://www.osha.gov/SLTC/etools/hospital/hazards/tb/tb.html
- Safety and Health Topics Page
  - *Tuberculosis*
    http://www.osha.gov/SLTC/tuberculosis/index.html

Physical Hazards and Others

Ionizing Radiation standard (29 CFR 1910.1096). Ionizing radiation sources may be found in a wide range of occupational settings, including, but not limited to, healthcare facilities, research institutions, nuclear reactors and their support facilities, nuclear weapons production facilities, and other various manufacturing settings. These radiation sources pose considerable health risks to affected workers if not properly controlled. This standard requires employers to conduct a survey of the types of radiation used in the facility, including x-rays, to designate restricted areas to limit worker exposure and to require those working in designated areas to wear personal radiation monitors. In addition, radiation areas and equipment must be labeled and equipped with caution signs.

- Complete standard
  - **29 CFR 1910.1096**
    http://www.osha.gov/pls/oshaweb/owadisp.show_document?p_table=STANDARDS&p_id=10098
- Safety and Health Topics Page
  - *Ionizing Radiation*
    http://www.osha.gov/SLTC/radiationionizing/index.html
- Hospital eTool
  - *Radiation Exposure*
    http://www.osha.gov/SLTC/etools/hospital/clinical/radiology/radiology.html#Radiation

Occupational Noise Exposure standard (29 CFR 1910.95). This standard requires employers to have a hearing conservation program in place if workers are exposed to a time-weighted average of 85 decibels (dB) over an 8-hour work shift.

- Complete standard
  - **29 CFR 1910.95**
    http://www.osha.gov/pls/oshaweb/owadisp.show_document?p_table=STANDARDS&p_id=10625
- Safety and Health Topics Page
  - *Noise and Hearing Conservation*
    http://www.osha.gov/SLTC/noisehearingconservation/index.html
- Fact Sheet
  - **Laboratory Safety – Noise**
    http://www.osha.gov/Publications/laboratory/OSHAfactsheet-laboratory-safety-noise.pdf

Additional OSHA Information on Physical Hazards

Centrifuges

- QuickFacts
  - *Laboratory Safety – Centrifuges.* OSHA Publication 3406 (2011).
    http://www.osha.gov/Publications/laboratory/OSHAquickfacts-lab-safety-centrifuges.pdf

Cryogens & Dry Ice

- QuickFacts
  - *Laboratory Safety – Cryogens & Dry Ice.* OSHA Publication 3408 (2011).
    http://www.osha.gov/Publications/laboratory/OSHAquickfacts-lab-safety-cryogens-dryice.pdf

Laser hazards

- Safety and Health Information Bulletin
  - *Hazard of Laser Surgery Smoke* (1988).
    http://www.osha.gov/dts/hib/hib_data/hib19880411.html

Occupational Safety and
Health Administration

- Hospital eTool
  - *Laser Hazards*
    http://www.osha.gov/SLTC/etools/hospital/surgical/lasers.html
- Safety and Health Topics Pages
  - *Laser Hazards*
    http://www.osha.gov/SLTC/laserhazards/index.html
  - *Laser/Electrosurgery Plume*
    http://www.osha.gov/SLTC/laserelectrosurgeryplume/index.html

Safety Hazards

The Control of Hazardous Energy standard (29 CFR 1910.147), often called the "Lockout/Tagout" standard, establishes basic requirements for locking and/or tagging out equipment while installation, maintenance, testing, repair, or construction operations are in progress. The primary purpose of the standard is to protect workers from the unexpected energization or start-up of machines or equipment, or release of stored energy.
- Complete standard
  - **29 CFR 1910.147**
    http://www.osha.gov/pls/oshaweb/owadisp.show_document?p_table=STANDARDS&p_id=9804
- Booklet
  - *Control of Hazardous Energy Lockout/Tagout*. OSHA Publication 3120 (2002).
    http://www.osha.gov/Publications/osha3120.pdf
- Safety and Health Topics Page
  - *Control of Hazardous Energy (Lockout/Tagout)*
    http://www.osha.gov/SLTC/controlhazardousenergy/index.html

Electrical Hazards standards (29 CFR 1910 Subpart S). Wiring deficiencies are one of the hazards most frequently cited by OSHA. OSHA's electrical standards include design requirements for electrical systems and safety-related work practices. If flammable gases are used, special wiring and equipment installation may be required.
- Complete standard
  - **29 CFR 1910 Subpart S**
    http://www.osha.gov/pls/oshaweb/owadisp.show_document?p_table=STANDARDS&p_id=10135
- Booklet
  - *Controlling Electrical Hazards*. OSHA Publication 3075 (2002).
    http://www.osha.gov/Publications/osha3075.pdf
- Safety and Health Topics Page
  - *Electrical*
    http://www.osha.gov/SLTC/electrical/index.html
- Hospital eTool
  - *Electrical Hazards*
    http://www.osha.gov/SLTC/etools/hospital/hazards/electrical/electrical.html
- QuickFacts
  - *Laboratory Safety – Electrical Hazards*. OSHA Publication 3409 (2011).
    http://www.osha.gov/Publications/laboratory/OSHAquickfacts-lab-safety-electrical-hazards.pdf

Fire Prevention Plans standard (29 CFR 1910.39). OSHA recommends that all employers have a Fire Prevention Plan. A plan is mandatory when required by an OSHA standard. Additional fire hazard information is available via OSHA publications and web pages.
- Complete standard
  - **29 CFR 1910.39**
    http://www.osha.gov/pls/oshaweb/owadisp.show_document?p_table=STANDARDS&p_id=12887
- Booklet
  - *Fire Service Features of Buildings and Fire Protection Systems*. OSHA Publication 3256 (2006).
    http://www.osha.gov/Publications/osha3256.pdf
- Expert Advisor
  - *Fire Safety Advisor*
    http://www.osha.gov/dts/osta/oshasoft/softfirex.html

- Fact Sheet
  - ***Fire Safety in the Workplace***
    http://www.osha.gov/OshDoc/data_General_Facts/FireSafetyN.pdf
- Safety and Health Topics Page
  - ***Fire Safety***
    http://www.osha.gov/SLTC/firesafety/index.html
- eTool
  - ***Evacuation Plans and Procedures***
    http://www.osha.gov/SLTC/etools/evacuation/index.html

Additional OSHA Information on Safety Hazards
Compressed gas
- Safety and Health Topics Page
  - ***Compressed Gas and Equipment***
    http://www.osha.gov/SLTC/compressedgasequipment/index.html
Ergonomics
- Fact Sheet
  - ***Laboratory Safety – Ergonomics for the Prevention of Musculoskeletal Disorders***
    http://www.osha.gov/Publications/laboratory/OSHAfactsheet-laboratory-safety-ergonomics.pdf

Engineering Controls
Autoclaves/Sterilizers
- QuickFacts
  - ***Laboratory Safety – Autoclaves/Sterilizers.*** OSHA Publication 3405 (2011).
    http://www.osha.gov/Publications/laboratory/OSHAquickfacts-lab-safety-autoclaves-sterilizers.pdf
Biosafety Cabinets (BSCs)
- Fact Sheet
  - ***Laboratory Safety – Biosafety Cabinets (BSCs).***
    http://www.osha.gov/Publications/laboratory/OSHAfactsheet-laboratory-safety-biosafety-cabinets.pdf
Chemical Fume Hoods
- QuickFacts
  - ***Laboratory Safety – Chemical Fume Hoods.*** OSHA Publication 3407 (2011).
    http://www.osha.gov/Publications/laboratory/OSHAquickfacts-lab-safety-chemical-fume-hoods.pdf

Personal Protective Equipment
The Personal Protective Equipment (PPE) standard (29 CFR 1910.132) requires that employers provide PPE and ensure that it is used wherever "hazards of processes or environment, chemical hazards, radiological hazards, or mechanical irritants [are] encountered in a manner capable of causing injury or impairment in the function of any part of the body through absorption, inhalation or physical contact," 29 CFR 1910.132(a).
- Complete standards
  - **29 CFR 1910 Subpart I**
    http://www.osha.gov/pls/oshaweb/owadisp.show_document?p_table=STANDARDS&p_id=10118
- Fact Sheet
  - ***Personal Protective Equipment***
    http://www.osha.gov/OshDoc/data_General_Facts/ppe-factsheet.pdf
- Brochures/Booklets
  - ***Personal Protective Equipment.*** OSHA Publication 3151 (2003).
    http://www.osha.gov/Publications/osha3151.html
- Safety and Health Topics Page
  - ***Personal Protective Equipment***
    http://www.osha.gov/SLTC/personalprotectiveequipment/index.html

The Eye and Face Protection standard (29 CFR 1910.133) requires that employers ensure that each affected employee uses appropriate eye or face protection when exposed to eye or face hazards from flying

Occupational Safety and
Health Administration

particles, molten metal, liquid chemicals, acids or caustic liquids, chemical gases or vapors, or potentially injurious light radiation, 29 CFR 1910.133(a).
- Complete standard
  - **29 CFR 1910.133**
    http://www.osha.gov/pls/oshaweb/owadisp.show_document?p_table=STANDARDS&p_id=9778
- eTool
  - *Eye and Face Protection*
    http://www.osha.gov/SLTC/etools/eyeandface/index.html
- Safety and Health Topics Page
  - *Eye and Face Protection*
    http://www.osha.gov/SLTC/eyefaceprotection/index.html

The Respiratory Protection standard (29 CFR 1910.134) requires that a respirator be provided to each worker when such equipment is necessary to protect their health. The employer must provide respirators that are appropriate based on the hazards to which the worker is exposed and factors that affect respirator performance and reliability, as described in 29 CFR 1910.134(d)(1).
- Complete standard
  - **29 CFR 1910.134**
    http://www.osha.gov/pls/oshaweb/owadisp.show_document?p_table=STANDARDS&p_id=12716&p_text_version=FALSE
- Guidance Documents
  - *Respiratory Protection.* OSHA Publication 3079 (2002).
  - *Small Entity Compliance Guide for OSHA's Respiratory Protection Standard.* OSHA Publication 9071 (1999).
    http://www.osha.gov/Publications/secgrev-current.pdf
  - *Assigned Protection Factors for the Revised Respiratory Protection Standard.* OSHA Publication 3352 (2009).
    http://www.osha.gov/SLTC/etools/respiratory/index.html
- Fact Sheet
  - *Respiratory Infection Control: Respirators Versus Surgical Masks*
- eTool
  - *Respiratory Protection*
    http://www.osha.gov/SLTC/etools/respiratory/index.html
- Safety and Health Topics Page
  - *Respiratory Protection*
    http://www.osha.gov/SLTC/respiratoryprotection/index.html

The Hand Protection standard (29 CFR 1910.138), requires that employers select and require workers to use appropriate hand protection when their hands are exposed to hazards such as those from skin absorption of harmful substances; severe cuts or lacerations; severe abrasions; punctures; chemical burns; thermal burns; and harmful temperature extremes, 29 CFR 1910.138(a). Further, employers must base the selection of the appropriate hand protection on an evaluation of the performance characteristics of the hand protection relative to the task(s) to be performed, conditions present, duration of use, and the hazards and potential hazards identified, 29 CFR 1910.138(b).
- Complete standard
  - **29 CFR 1910.138**
    http://www.osha.gov/pls/oshaweb/owadisp.show_document?p_table=STANDARDS&p_id=9788

Miscellaneous Information
Emergency Action Plan standard (29 CFR 1910.38). OSHA recommends that all employers have an Emergency Action Plan. A plan is mandatory when required by an OSHA standard. An Emergency Action Plan describes the actions workers should take to ensure their safety in a fire or other emergency situation.
- Complete standard
  - **29 CFR 1910.38**
    http://www.osha.gov/pls/oshaweb/owadisp.show_document?p_table=STANDARDS&p_id=9726

- Brochures/Booklets
  - ■ *Principal Emergency Response and Preparedness – Requirements and Guidance.* OSHA Publication 3122 (2004) http://www.osha.gov/Publications/osha3122.pdf
  - ■ *How to Plan for Workplace Emergencies and Evacuations.* OSHA Publication 3088 (2001). http://www.osha.gov/Publications/osha3088.pdf
- QuickFacts
  - ■ *Laboratory Safety – Working with Small Animals.* OSHA Publication 3412 (2011). http://www.osha.gov/Publications/laboratory/OSHAquickfacts-lab-safety-working-with-small-animals.pdf
- eTool
  - ■ *Evacuation Plans and Procedures* http://www.osha.gov/SLTC/etools/evacuation/index.html
- eTool
  - ■ *Emergency Preparedness and Response* http://www.osha.gov/SLTC/emergencypreparedness/index.html

Exit Routes standards (29 CFR 1910.34 – 29 CFR 1910.37). All employers must comply with OSHA's requirements for exit routes in the workplace.
- Complete standards
  - ■ **29 CFR 1910.34** http://www.osha.gov/pls/oshaweb/owadisp.show_document?p_table=STANDARDS&p_id=12886
  - ■ **29 CFR 1910.35** http://www.osha.gov/pls/oshaweb/owadisp.show_document?p_table=STANDARDS&p_id=9723
  - ■ **29 CFR 1910.36** http://www.osha.gov/pls/oshaweb/owadisp.show_document?p_table=STANDARDS&p_id=9724
  - ■ **29 CFR 1910.37** http://www.osha.gov/pls/oshaweb/owadisp.show_document?p_table=STANDARDS&p_id=9725
- Fact Sheet
  - ■ *Emergency Exit Routes.* http://www.osha.gov/OshDoc/data_General_Facts/emergency-exit-routes-factsheet.pdf
- QuickCard™
  - ■ *Emergency Exit Routes.* OSHA Publication 3183 (2003).

Medical and First Aid standard (29 CFR 1910.151). OSHA requires employers to provide medical and first-aid personnel and supplies commensurate with the hazards of the workplace. The details of a workplace medical and first-aid program are dependent on the circumstances of each workplace and employer.
- Complete standard
  - ■ **29 CFR 1910.151** http://www.osha.gov/pls/oshaweb/owadisp.show_document?p_table=STANDARDS&p_id=9806
- Brochures/Booklets
  - ■ *Best Practices Guide: Fundamentals of a Workplace First-Aid Program.* OSHA Publication 3317 (2006) http://www.osha.gov/Publications/OSHA3317first-aid.pdf
- Safety and Health Topics Page
  - ■ *Medical and First Aid* http://www.osha.gov/SLTC/medicalfirstaid/index.html

Recordkeeping standard (29 CFR 1904). OSHA requires most employers to keep records of workplace injuries and illnesses. The employer should first determine if it is exempt from the routine recordkeeping requirements. An employer is not required to keep OSHA injury and illness records (unless asked to do so in writing by OSHA or the Bureau of Labor Statistics) if:
- It had 10 or fewer workers during all of the last calendar year (29 CFR 1904.1); or
- It is engaged in certain low-hazard industries (29 CFR Part 1904, Subpart B, Appendix A). The following types of healthcare facilities are exempt from OSHA's injury and illness recordkeeping requirements, regardless of size:
  - ■ Offices and Clinics of Medical Doctors (SIC 801)
  - ■ Offices and Clinics of Dentists (SIC 802)
  - ■ Offices of Osteopathic Physicians (SIC 803)

- Offices of Other Health Care Practitioners (SIC 804)
- Medical and Dental Laboratories (SIC 807)
- Health and Allied Services, Not Elsewhere Classified (SIC 809)

If an employer does not fall within one of these exemptions, it must comply with OSHA's recordkeeping requirements. Download OSHA's recordkeeping forms or order them from the OSHA Publications Office at www.osha.gov.

For additional information on the Recordkeeping standard, see the following OSHA documents.
- Complete standards
  - ***Recording and reporting occupational injuries and illness.*** 29 CFR 1904
    http://www.osha.gov/pls/oshaweb/owasrch.search_form?p_doc_type=STANDARDS&p_toc_level=1&p_keyvalue=1904
  - ***Recording criteria for needlestick and sharps injuries.*** 29 CFR 1904.8
    http://www.osha.gov/pls/oshaweb/owadisp.show_document?p_table=STANDARDS&p_id=9639
- Standard Interpretations
  - ***Recordkeeping Handbook - The Regulation and Related Interpretations for Recording and Reporting Occupational Injuries and Illnesses.*** OSHA Publication 3245 (2005).
    http://www.osha.gov/recordkeeping/handbook/index.html
- Fact Sheets
  - ***Highlights of OSHA's Recordkeeping Rule***
    http://www.osha.gov/OshDoc/data_RecordkeepingFacts/RKfactsheet1.pdf
  - ***OSHA Recordkeeping Help***
    http://www.osha.gov/OshDoc/data_RecordkeepingFacts/RKfactsheet2.pdf
- Brochures
  - ***Access to Medical and Exposure Records.*** OSHA Publication 3110 (2001).
    http://www.osha.gov/Publications/osha3110.pdf
  - ***RECORDKEEPING - It's new, it's improved, and it's easier....*** OSHA Publication 3169 (2001).
    http://www.osha.gov/Publications/osha3169.pdf
  - ***Recordkeeping Handbook.*** OSHA Publication 3245 (2005).
    http://www.osha.gov/Publications/osha3245.pdf
- OSHA Web Page
  - ***Injury and Illness: Recordkeeping***
    http://www.osha.gov/recordkeeping/index.html

Access to Worker Exposure and Medical Records standard (29 CFR 1910.1020).
This standard requires all employers, regardless of size or industry, to report the work-related death of any worker or hospitalizations of three or more workers. It also requires employers to provide workers, their designated representatives, and OSHA with access to worker exposure and medical records. Employers generally should maintain worker exposure records for 30 years and medical records for the duration of the worker's employment plus 30 years, unless one of the exemptions listed in 29 CFR 1910.1020(d)(1)(i) (A)-(C) applies.

All employers covered by OSHA recordkeeping requirements must post the OSHA Poster (or state plan equivalent) in a prominent location in the workplace. The OSHA Poster can be downloaded or ordered in either English or Spanish.

The following OSHA document provides more detailed information on this standard.
- Booklet
  - ***Access to Medical and Exposure Records.*** OSHA Publication 3110 (2001).
    http://www.osha.gov/Publications/osha3110.pdf

> NOTE: If your workplace is in a state operating an OSHA-approved state program, state plan record-keeping and reporting regulations, although substantially identical to federal ones, may have different exemptions or more stringent or supplemental requirements, such as for reporting of fatalities and catastrophes. Contact your state program directly for additional information.

Other Governmental and Non-governmental Agencies Involved in Laboratory Safety

U.S. Environmental Protection Agency (EPA)

Microbial Products of Biotechnology: Final Rule (62 FR 17910)

The regulation under which the TSCA Biotechnology Program functions is titled "Microbial Products of Biotechnology; Final Regulation Under the Toxic Substances Control Act" (TSCA), published in the Federal Register on April 11, 1997. This rule was developed under TSCA Section 5, which authorizes the Agency to, among other things, review new chemicals before they are introduced into commerce. Under a 1986 intergovernmental policy statement, intergeneric microorganisms (microorganisms created to contain genetic material from organisms in more than one taxonomic genus) are considered new chemicals under TSCA Section 5. The Biotechnology rule sets forth the manner in which the Agency will review and regulate the use of intergeneric microorganisms in commerce, or commercial research.

Documents relevant to this rule can be found at the following web site: http://www.epa.gov/oppt/biotech/pubs/biorule.htm.

U.S. Nuclear Regulatory Commission (NRC)

10 CFR 31.11 – General license for use of byproduct material for certain in vitro clinical or laboratory testing. Link at: http://www.nrc.gov/reading-rm/doc-collections/cfr/part031/part031-0011.html.

U.S. Department of Transportation (DOT)

An infectious substance is regulated as a hazardous material under the DOT's Hazardous Materials Regulations (HMR; 49 CFR Parts 171-180). The HMR apply to any material DOT determines is capable of posing an unreasonable risk to health, safety, and property when transported in commerce. An infectious substance must conform to all applicable HMR requirements when offered for transportation or transported by air, highway, rail, or water.

DOT's Pipeline and Hazardous Materials Safety Administration (PHMSA) published a final rule on June 1, 2006, revising the requirements in the HMR applicable to the transportation of infectious substances. The new requirements became effective October 1, 2006. Changes under the new rule apply to parts 171, 172, 173, and 175 of the HMR and include the following:

- New classification system
- New and revised definitions
- Revised marking requirements
- Revised packaging requirements
- New shipping paper requirements
- New security plan requirements
- New carriage by aircraft requirements

A guide to these changes is available at: http://www.phmsa.dot.gov/staticfiles/PHMSA/ DownloadableFiles/Files/Transporting_Infectious_ Substances_brochure.pdf.

U.S. Department of Health and Human Services (HHS)

Centers for Disease Control and Prevention (CDC)
Biosafety Levels

Laboratory supervisors are responsible for ensuring that appropriate safety and health precautions are in place in the laboratory. Therefore, for each biosafety level, there are specific supervisory qualifications as assurance that laboratory workers are provided with effective supervision. Various types of specialized controls and equipment are used to provide primary barriers between the microorganism and the laboratory worker. These range from disposable gloves and other PPE to complex biosafety cabinets or other containment devices.

The laboratory director is specifically and primarily responsible for the safe operation of the laboratory. His/her knowledge and judgment are critical in assessing risks and appropriately applying these recommendations. The recommended biosafety level represents those conditions under which the agent can ordinarily be safely handled. Special characteristics of the agents used, the training and experience of personnel, and the nature or function of the laboratory may further influence the director in applying these recommendations.

The U.S. Department of Health and Human Services' (DHHS) Centers for Disease Control and Prevention (CDC) defines four levels of biosafety, which are outlined below. Selection of an appropriate biosafety level for work with a particular agent or animal study (see Animal Facilities) depends upon a number of factors. Some of the most important are the virulence, pathogenicity, biological stability, route of spread, and communicability of the agent; the nature or function of the laboratory; the procedures and manipulations involving the agent; the endemicity (restricted to a locality/region) of the agent; and the availability of effective vaccines or therapeutic measures.

CDC Summary of Recommended Biosafety Levels for Infectious Agents				
Biosafety Level	Agent Characteristics	Practices	Safety Equipment	Facilities (secondary barriers)
BSL-1	Not known to consistently cause disease in healthy adults	Standard microbiological Practices	None	Open bench top sink
BSL-2	Associated with human disease, hazard from percutaneous injury, ingestion, mucous membrane exposure	Standard microbiological Practices

Limited access

Biohazard warning signs

Sharps precautions

Biosafety manual defining any needed waste decontamination or medical surveillance policies. | Class I or II biosafety cabinets (BSCs) or other containment devices used for all agents that cause splashes or aerosols of infectious materials

Laboratory coats and gloves

Face protection as needed | Open bench top sink

Autoclave |
| BSL-3 | Indigenous or exotic agents with potential for aerosol transmission; disease may have serious or lethal consequences | All BSL-2 practices

Controlled access

Decontamination of all waste

Decontamination of laboratory clothing before laundering

Baseline serum | Class I or II BSCs or other physical containment devices used for all open manipulations of agents

Protective lab clothing and gloves

Respiratory protection as needed | Open bench top sink

Autoclave

Physical separation from access corridors

Self-closing, double-door access

Exhaust air not recirculated

Negative airflow in laboratory |
| BSL-4 | Dangerous/exotic agents which pose high risk of life-threatening disease; aerosol-transmitted lab infections; or related agents with unknown risk of transmission | All BSL-3 practices

Clothing change before entering

Shower on exit

All material decontaminated on exit from facility | All procedures conducted in Class III BSCs, or Class I or II BSCs in combination with full-body, air-supplied, positive pressure personnel suit. | BSL-3 plus:

Separate building or isolated zone

Dedicated supply and exhaust, vacuum, and decontamination systems

Other requirements outlined in the text |

NOTE: The following information has been adapted from *Biosafety in Microbiological and Biomedical Laboratories*, 5th Ed. (BMBL, 5th Ed.), which is published jointly by the U.S. Centers for Disease Control and Prevention (CDC) and the National Institutes of Health (NIH), and is available online at www.cdc.gov/od/ohs/biosfty/bmbl5/bmbl5toc.htm. Laboratory workers and supervisors are strongly urged to review this publication directly before engaging in any experimentation.

Biosafety Level 1 (BSL-1)

BSL-1 is appropriate for working with microorganisms that are not known to cause disease in healthy humans. BSL-I practices, safety equipment, and facility design and construction are appropriate for undergraduate and secondary educational training and teaching laboratories, and for other laboratories in which work is done with defined and characterized strains of viable microorganisms not known to consistently cause disease in healthy adult humans. *Bacillus subtilis, Naegleria gruberi*, infectious canine hepatitis virus, and exempt organisms under the *NIH Recombinant DNA Guidelines* (http://www4.od nih.gov/oba/rac/guidelines/guidelines.html) are representative of microorganisms meeting these criteria. Many agents not ordinarily associated with disease processes in humans are, however, opportunistic pathogens and may cause infection in the young, the aged, and immunodeficient or immunosuppressed individuals. Vaccine strains that have undergone multiple in vivo passages should not be considered avirulent simply because they are vaccine strains.

BSL-1 represents a basic level of containment that relies on standard microbiological practices with no special primary or secondary barriers recommended, other than a sink for hand washing.

Biosafety Level 2 (BSL-2)

The facility, containment devices, administrative controls, and practices and procedures that constitute BSL-2 are designed to maximize safe working conditions for laboratory personnel working with agents of moderate risk to personnel and the environment. BSL-2 practices, equipment, and facility design and construction are applicable to clinical, diagnostic, teaching, and other laboratories in which work is done with the broad spectrum of indigenous moderate-risk agents that are present in the community and associated with human disease of varying severity. With good microbiological techniques, these agents can be used safely in activities conducted on the open bench, provided the potential for producing splashes or

aerosols is low. Hepatitis B virus, H1V, the salmonellae, and Toxoplasma spp. are representative of microorganisms assigned to this containment level.

Biosafety Level 2 is also appropriate when work is done with any human-derived blood, body fluids, tissues, or primary human cell lines where the presence of an infectious agent may be unknown. Laboratory personnel in the United States working with human-derived materials should refer to the U.S. Occupational Safety and Health Administration (OSHA) *Bloodborne Pathogens Standard* (OSHA 1991), available online at www.osha.gov/pls/oshaweb/owadisp.show_document?p_table=STANDARDS7p_id=1005, for required precautions.

Primary hazards to personnel working with these agents relate to accidental percutaneous or mucous membrane exposures, or ingestion of infectious materials. Extreme caution should be taken with contaminated needles or sharp instruments. Even though organisms routinely manipulated at Biosafety Level 2 are not known to be transmissible by the aerosol route, procedures with aerosol or high splash potential that may increase the risk of such personnel exposure must be conducted in primary containment equipment, or in devices such as a biological safety cabinet (BSC) or safety centrifuge cups. Personal protective equipment (PPE) should be used as appropriate, such as splash shields, face protection, gowns, and gloves.

Secondary barriers such as hand washing sinks and waste decontamination facilities must be available to reduce potential environmental contamination.

Biosafety Level 3 (BSL-3)

BSL-3 is suitable for work with infectious agents which may cause serious or potentially lethal diseases as a result of exposure by the inhalation route. This may apply to clinical, diagnostic, teaching, research, or production facilities in which work is done with indigenous or exotic agents with potential for respiratory transmission, and which may cause serious and potentially lethal infection. *Mycobacterium tuberculosis*, St. Louis encephalitis virus, and *Coxiella burnetti* are representative of the microorganisms assigned to this level. Primary hazards to personnel working with these agents relate to autoinoculation, ingestion, and exposure to infectious aerosols.

At BSL-3, more emphasis is placed on primary and secondary barriers to protect personnel in contiguous

areas, the community, and the environment from exposure to potentially infectious aerosols. For example, all laboratory manipulations should be performed in a BSC or other enclosed equipment, such as a gas-tight aerosol generation chamber. Secondary barriers for this level include controlled access to the laboratory and ventilation requirements that minimize the release of infectious aerosols from the laboratory.

Biosafety Level 4 (BSL-4)

BSL-4 practices, safety equipment, and facility design and construction are applicable for work with dangerous and exotic agents that pose a high individual risk of life-threatening disease, which may be transmitted via the aerosol route, and for which there is no available vaccine or therapy. Agents with a close or identical antigenic relationship to Biosafety Level 4 agents also should be handled at this level. When sufficient data are obtained, work with these agents may continue at this or at a lower level. Viruses such as Marburg or Congo-Crimean hemorrhagic fever are manipulated at Biosafety Level 4.

The primary hazards to personnel working with Biosafety Level 4 agents are respiratory exposure to infectious aerosols, mucous membrane or broken skin exposure to infectious droplets, and autoinoculation. All manipulations of potentially infectious diagnostic materials, isolates, and naturally or experimentally infected animals pose a high risk of exposure and infection to laboratory personnel, the community, and the environment.

The laboratory worker's complete isolation from aerosolized infectious materials is accomplished primarily by working in a Class III BSC or in a full-body, air-supplied, positive-pressure personnel suit. The BSL-4 facility itself is generally a separate building or completely isolated zone with complex, specialized ventilation requirements and waste management systems to prevent release of viable agents to the environment.

Animal Biosafety Levels

The CDC defines four biosafety levels for activities involving infectious disease work with experimental animals. These combinations of practices, safety equipment, and facilities are designated Animal Biosafety Levels 1, 2, 3, and 4, and provide increasing levels of protection to personnel and the environment.

Protocols using live animals must first be reviewed and approved by an Institutional Animal Care and Use Committee (IACUC) or must conform to governmen-

tal regulations regarding the care and use of laboratory animals. Follow all appropriate guidelines for the use and handling of infected animals.

For more information, refer to Section V of the BMBL, 5th Ed., available online at www.cdc.gov/od/ohs/biosafty/bmbl5/bmbl5toc.htm.

National Institutes of Health (NIH)

The NIH Office of Biotechnology Activities (OBA) promotes science, safety, and ethics in biotechnology through advancement of knowledge, enhancement of public understanding, and development of sound public policies. OBA accomplishes its mission through analysis, deliberation, and communication of scientific, medical, ethical, legal, and social issues.

OBA fulfills its mission through four important programs:
- Recombinant DNA (RAC)
- Genetics, Health, Society (SACGHS)
- Dual Use Research (NSABB)
- Clinical Research Policy Analysis and Coordination (CRpac)

Links to each of the programs listed above are provided at the OBA website: http://oba.od.nih.gov/oba/index.html.

National Institute for Occupational Safety and Health (NIOSH)

The NIOSH **Pocket Guide to Chemical Hazards (NPG)** (available at: www.cdc.gov/niosh/npg) provides a source of general industrial hygiene information on several hundred chemicals/classes for workers, employers, and occupational health professionals. While the NPG does not contain an analysis of all pertinent data, it presents key information and data in abbreviated or tabular form for chemicals or substance groupings (e.g., cyanides, fluorides, manganese compounds) that are found in the work environment. The information contained in the NPG should help users recognize and control occupational chemical hazards.

Other Government Web Links for Access to Additional Information Concerning Laboratory Safety

The Animal Plant Health Inspection Service (APHIS), www.usda/aphis.gov

U.S. Department of Agriculture (USDA), www.usda.gov

National Institute for Occupational Safety and Health (NIOSH), www.niosh.gov

U.S. Department of Health and Human Services (DHHS), www.hhs.gov

U.S. Department of Transportation (DOT), www.dot.gov

U.S. Food and Drug Administration (FDA), www.fda.gov

Government Regulatory Agency Web Links

Code of Federal Regulations Search Engine, www.access.gpo.gov/nara/cfr/index.html

Environmental Protection Agency, www.epa.gov

Federal Register Search Engine, www.access.gpo.gov/su_docs/aces/aces140.html

Food and Drug Administration, www.fda.gov

Nuclear Regulatory Commission, www.nrc.gov

Occupational Safety and Health Administration (OSHA), www.osha.gov

Non-governmental Agency Web Links for Access to Additional Information Concerning Laboratory Safety

American Biological Safety Association (ABSA), www.absa.org

College of American Pathologists (CAP), www.cap.org

Institute for Laboratory Animal Research (ILAR), www.dels.nas.edu/ilar_n/ilarhome

National Fire Protection Association (NFPA), www.nfpa.org

Dictionary of Safety Terms

Oregon OSHA Dictionary of Safety Terms - Spanish to English, www.orosha.org/pdf/dictionary/spanish-english.pdf

Oregon OSHA Dictionary of Safety Terms - English to Spanish, www.orosha.org/pdf/dictionary/english-spanish.pdf

Most Common Zoonotic Diseases in Workers

Workers that work with animals may be exposed to a number of zoonotic diseases. Examples of some of the zoonotic diseases that workers may be exposed to are listed in the table below.

Disease	Disease agent	Animals				
		Cats	Dogs	Birds	Farm Animals	Wild Animals
Brucellosis	*Brucella canis*		X			
Campylobacteriosis	*Campylobacter jejuni*	X	X		X	
Cat Scratch Fever	*Bartonella henselae*	X				
Cryptococcosis	*Cryptococcus neoformans* and other species			X		
Hemorrhagic fever with renal syndrome (HFRS) and hantavirus pulmonary syndrome (HPS)	Hantavirus					X
Lymphocytic choriomeningitis	Lymphocytic choriomeningitis virus (LCMV)			X		
Pasteurella pneumonia	*Pasteurella haemolytica*				X	
Histoplasmosis	*Histoplasma capsulatum*			X		
Orf	Poxvirus				X	
Plague	*Yersinia pestis*					X
Q-fever	*Coxiella burnetii*				X	
Rabies	Rabies virus	X	X			
Salmonellosis	*Salmonella enterica* serovar Typhi				X	
Toxoplasmosis	*Toxoplasma gondii*	X				
Tularemia	*Tularemia francisella*					X

Complaints, Emergencies and Further Assistance

Workers have the right to a safe workplace. The *Occupational Safety and Health Act of 1970* (OSH Act) was passed to prevent workers from being killed or seriously harmed at work. The law requires employers to provide their employees with working conditions that are free of known dangers. Workers may file a complaint to have OSHA inspect their workplace if they believe that their employer is not following OSHA standards or that there are serious hazards. Further, the Act gives complainants the right to request that their names not be revealed to their employers. It is also against the law for an employer to fire, demote, transfer, or discriminate in any way against a worker for filing a complaint or using other OSHA rights.

To report an emergency, file a complaint, or seek OSHA advice, assistance, or products, call (800) 321-OSHA (6742) or contact your nearest OSHA regional, area, or state plan office listed or linked to at the end of this publication. The teletypewriter (TTY) number is (877) 889-5627. You can also file a complaint online by visiting OSHA's website at www.osha.gov. Most complaints submitted online may be resolved informally over the phone or by fax with your employer. Written complaints, that are signed by a worker or their representative and submitted to the closest OSHA office, are more likely to result in an on-site OSHA inspection.

Compliance Assistance Resources

OSHA can provide extensive help through a variety of programs, including free workplace consultations, compliance assistance, voluntary protection programs, strategic partnerships, alliances, and training and education. For more information on any of the programs listed below, visit OSHA's website at www.osha.gov or call 1-800-321-OSHA (6742).

Establishing an Injury and Illness Prevention Program

The key to a safe and healthful work environment is a comprehensive injury and illness prevention program.

Injury and illness prevention programs, known by a variety of names, are universal interventions that can substantially reduce the number and severity of workplace injuries and alleviate the associated financial burdens on U.S. workplaces. Many states have requirements or voluntary guidelines for workplace injury and illness prevention programs. In addition, numerous employers in the United States already manage safety using injury and illness prevention programs, and we believe that all employers can and should do the same. Employers in the construction industry are already required to have a health and safety program. Most successful injury and illness prevention programs are based on a common set of key elements. These include management leadership, worker participation, hazard identification, hazard prevention and control, education and training, and program evaluation and improvement. Visit OSHA's website at http://www.osha.gov/dsg/topics/safetyhealth/index.html for more information and guidance on establishing effective injury and illness prevention programs in the workplace.

Compliance Assistance Specialists

OSHA has compliance assistance specialists throughout the nation who can provide information to employers and workers about OSHA standards, short educational programs on specific hazards or OSHA rights and responsibilities, and information on additional compliance assistance resources. Contact your local OSHA office for more information.

OSHA Consultation Service for Small Employers

The OSHA Consultation Service provides **free assistance** to small employers to help them identify and correct hazards, and to improve their injury and illness prevention programs. Most of these services are delivered on site by state government agencies or universities using well-trained professional staff.

Consultation services are available to private sector employers. Priority is given to small employers with the most hazardous operations or in the most high-hazard industries. These programs are largely funded by OSHA and are delivered at no cost to employers who request help. Consultation services are separate from enforcement activities. To request such services, an employer can phone or write to the OSHA Consultation Program. See the Small Business section of OSHA's website for contact information for the consultation offices in every state.

- **Safety and Health Achievement Recognition Program**
  Under the consultation program, certain exemplary employers may request participation in OSHA's Safety and Health Achievement

Occupational Safety and Health Administration

Recognition Program (SHARP). Eligibility for participation includes, but is not limited to, receiving a full-service, comprehensive consultation visit, correcting all identified hazards, and developing an effective injury and illness prevention program.

Cooperative Programs

OSHA offers cooperative programs to help prevent fatalities, injuries and illnesses in the workplace.

- **OSHA's Alliance Program**

  Through the Alliance Program, OSHA works with groups committed to worker safety and health to prevent workplace fatalities, injuries, and illnesses. These groups include businesses, trade or professional organizations, unions, consulates, faith- and community-based organizations, and educational institutions. OSHA and the groups work together to develop compliance assistance tools and resources, share information with workers and employers, and educate workers and employers about their rights and responsibilities.

- **Challenge Program**

  This program helps employers and workers improve their injury and illness prevention programs and implement an effective system to prevent fatalities, injuries and illnesses.

- **OSHA Strategic Partnership Program (OSPP)**

  Partnerships are formalized through tailored agreements designed to encourage, assist and recognize partner efforts to eliminate serious hazards and achieve model workplace safety and health practices.

- **Voluntary Protection Programs (VPP)**

  The VPP recognize employers and workers in private industry and federal agencies who have implemented effective injury and illness prevention programs and maintain injury and illness rates below national Bureau of Labor Statistics averages for their respective industries. In VPP, management, labor, and OSHA work cooperatively and proactively to prevent fatalities, injuries, and illnesses.

OSHA Training Institute Education Centers

The OSHA Training Institute (OTI) Education Centers are a national network of nonprofit organizations authorized by OSHA to conduct occupational safety and health training to private sector workers, supervisors and employers.

Susan Harwood Training and Education Grants

OSHA provides grants to nonprofit organizations to provide worker education and training on serious job hazards and avoidance/prevention strategies.

Information and Publications

OSHA has a variety of educational materials and electronic tools available on its website at www.osha.gov. These include Safety and Health Topics Pages, Safety Fact Sheets, Expert Advisor software, copies of regulations and compliance directives, videos and other information for employers and workers. OSHA's software programs and eTools walk you through safety and health issues and common problems to find the best solutions for your workplace.

OSHA's extensive publications help explain OSHA standards, job hazards, and mitigation strategies and provide assistance in developing injury and illness prevention programs.

For a listing of free publications, visit OSHA's website at www.osha.gov or call 1-800-321-OSHA (6742).

QuickTakes

OSHA's free, twice monthly online newsletter, *QuickTakes*, offers the latest news about OSHA initiatives and products to assist employers and workers in finding and preventing workplace hazards. To sign up for *QuickTakes*, visit OSHA's website at www.osha.gov and click on *QuickTakes* at the top of the page.

Contacting OSHA

To order additional copies of this publication, to get a list of other OSHA publications, to ask questions or to get more information, to contact OSHA's free consultation service, or to file a confidential complaint, contact OSHA at 1-800-321-OSHA (6742), (TTY) 1-877-889-5627 or visit www.osha.gov.

**For assistance, contact us.
We are OSHA. We can help.
It's confidential.**

OSHA Regional Offices

Region I
Boston Regional Office
(CT*, ME, MA, NH, RI, VT*)
JFK Federal Building, Room E340
Boston, MA 02203
(617) 565-9860 (617) 565-9827 Fax

Region II
New York Regional Office
(NJ*, NY*, PR*, VI*)
201 Varick Street, Room 670
New York, NY 10014
(212) 337-2378 (212) 337-2371 Fax

Region III
Philadelphia Regional Office
(DE, DC, MD*, PA, VA*, WV)
The Curtis Center
170 S. Independence Mall West
Suite 740 West
Philadelphia, PA 19106-3309
(215) 861-4900 (215) 861-4904 Fax

Region IV
Atlanta Regional Office
(AL, FL, GA, KY*, MS, NC*, SC*, TN*)
61 Forsyth Street, SW, Room 6T50
Atlanta, GA 30303
(678) 237-0400 (678) 237-0447 Fax

Region V
Chicago Regional Office
(IL*, IN*, MI*, MN*, OH, WI)
230 South Dearborn Street
Room 3244
Chicago, IL 60604
(312) 353-2220 (312) 353-7774 Fax

Region VI
Dallas Regional Office
(AR, LA, NM*, OK, TX)
525 Griffin Street, Room 602
Dallas, TX 75202
(972) 850-4145 (972) 850-4149 Fax
(972) 850-4150 FSO Fax

Region VII
Kansas City Regional Office
(IA*, KS, MO, NE)
Two Pershing Square Building
2300 Main Street, Suite 1010
Kansas City, MO 64108-2416
(816) 283-8745 (816) 283-0547 Fax

Region VIII
Denver Regional Office
(CO, MT, ND, SD, UT*, WY*)
1999 Broadway, Suite 1690
Denver, CO 80202
(720) 264-6550 (720) 264-6585 Fax

Region IX
San Francisco Regional Office
(AZ*, CA*, HI*, NV*, and American Samoa,
Guam and the Northern Mariana Islands)
90 7th Street, Suite 18100
San Francisco, CA 94103
(415) 625-2547 (415) 625-2534 Fax

Region X
Seattle Regional Office
(AK*, ID, OR*, WA*)
300 Fifth Avenue, Suite 1280
Seattle, WA 98104-2397
(206) 757-6700 (206) 757-6705 Fax

*These states and territories operate their own OSHA-approved job safety and health plans and cover state and local government employees as well as private sector employees. The Connecticut, Illinois, New Jersey, New York and Virgin Islands programs cover public employees only. (Private sector workers in these states are covered by Federal OSHA). States with approved programs must have standards that are identical to, or at least as effective as, the Federal OSHA standards.

Note: To get contact information for OSHA area offices, OSHA-approved state plan offices and OSHA consultation projects, please visit us online at www.osha.gov or call us at 1-800-321-OSHA (6742).

OSHA
Occupational Safety and
Health Administration